© 2025 by Randolph Simmons.
ISBN: 979-8-9929844-0-8

All rights reserved. This book or any portion thereof may not be reproduced or used in any manner whatsoever without the express written permission of the author, except for the use of brief quotations in a book review or scholarly journal.

Edited by: Sharp Editorial
Production Design by: Chynna Creative Co.

NO MORE EXCUSES

MASTERING THE SKILL OF
SELF- DISCIPLINE & EXECUTION

RANDOLPH "RANDY NOEXCUSE" SIMMONS

DEDICATION

To my sister, **Clarise Simmons** — My soldier, my rock, my #1 supporter. Thank you for always hyping me up, believing in me, and holding me down, no matter how far apart we are. Your constant love and loyalty gave me strength when I needed it most. This one's for you.

ACKNOWLEDGMENTS

This book would not have come to life without the guidance, support, and belief of a few key people.

To **Erica Berman** and **Erin Larson** — Thank you for your unwavering encouragement throughout the writing process. Your support kept me grounded and focused every step of the journey.

To the **Laci Swann & the Sharp Editorial team and Chynna Denny** — Your precision, professionalism, and commitment to excellence turned my vision into reality. Thank you for rolling with me through the crazy deadlines and believing in this project as much as I did. I'm deeply grateful for all of you. Thank you for being part of something that's bigger than a book—it's a movement.

Dear God,

Thank You for the lessons You've planned for my life—the victories, losses, pain, and growth. Thank You for giving me the opportunity to share these lessons, not just as words on a page but as real experiences that have shaped me into the man I am today. I ask that You bless this book. More importantly, please bless the reader.

God, I pray that whoever picks up this book reads it with an open heart and mind. Give them the courage to face the truth, to challenge themselves, and to embrace the changes they need to make. Tear down the mask they've been hiding behind. Tear down the walls they've built to protect themselves that keep them from growing. Remove the survival tactics that once kept them safe but now hold them back. Allow them to see themselves fully, accept where they are, and boldly step into the person You created them to be.

Let this book be more than words. Let it be a spark, a shift, and a wake-up call. Let these lessons push them to act, break free from the cycles that have kept them stuck, and chase after the lives they were meant to live. Help them to stop making excuses and doubting themselves and to move forward with faith, discipline, and purpose.

God, remind them that they are capable, strong, and never alone. Walk with them as they grow, heal, and step into the best version of themselves. Let this journey be one that brings them closer to You, their purpose, and the life they deserve.

Thank You for this moment. Thank You for their lives, and thank You for what's about to come.

In Jesus' name, Amen.

TABLE OF CONTENTS

CHAPTER ONE: NO EXCUSES, NO ESCAPE: FACING THE TRUTH & OWNING YOUR LIFE 1

CHAPTER TWO: UNDERSTANDING YOUR WHY 46

CHAPTER THREE: ALIGNING ACTIONS WITH PURPOSE 55

CHAPTER FOUR: OVERCOMING SETBACKS AND STAYING MOTIVATED 60

CHAPTER FIVE: STAYING TRUE TO YOUR PURPOSE DESPITE EXTERNAL PRESSURES 66

CHAPTER SIX: EMBRACING DISCOMFORT AND HARD WORK 70

CHAPTER SEVEN: BUILDING MENTAL TOUGHNESS 92

CHAPTER EIGHT: THE FOUNDATION OF SELF-DISCIPLINE 111

CHAPTER NINE: RADICAL ACCOUNTABILITY 130

CHAPTER TEN: CREATING A ROUTINE THAT ALIGNS WITH YOUR GOALS 153

CHAPTER ELEVEN: SEPARATING THE COMMITTED FROM THE COMFORTABLE 165

CHAPTER TWELVE: SURROUNDING YOURSELF WITH THE RIGHT PEOPLE 185

CHAPTER THIRTEEN: TURNING SETBACKS INTO SETUPS 202

CHAPTER FOURTEEN: LIVING THE EXCUSE KILLER LIFESTYLE 217

CHAPTER ONE: NO EXCUSES, NO ESCAPE: FACING THE TRUTH & OWNING YOUR LIFE

PART I: THE REALITY OF EXCUSES

Excuses are the easiest safety net to fall back on. Excuses are like quicksand—once you step into them, you sink deeper and deeper. People get comfortable in their excuses, blaming everything from time to circumstances, pushing off acting with thoughts like, "I'll start tomorrow," or "I don't have what it takes yet." These excuses sound small, but they slowly block the path to opportunities waiting on the other side.

For those who don't know me, my name is Randolph, though everyone calls me Randy. My nickname "Randy Savage" came from my boys, inspired by the wrestler Randy "Macho Man" Savage. When

I started acting out, Savage became more than a nickname but an alter ego. Born in Newark, New Jersey, my life wasn't set up for success from the start. My father worked in housekeeping at St. Michael's Medical Center, the same hospital where I was born. My mom, who worked as a kindergarten teacher at Full Gospel Christian Academy in Newark, didn't want me to go to school in Newark because she thought I'd end up fighting too much, which led our family to bounce between living in Newark and East Orange. That's how I ended up going to Cicely Tyson School of Performing Arts in East Orange, New Jersey.

Growing up, we didn't have much. For years, my family and I slept on the floor because we couldn't afford beds. I was used to rocking hand-me-downs and seeing kids at school wearing fresh Jordans and new clothes and spending extra lunch money. I felt like I was on the outside looking in. Embarrassment and the feeling of not measuring up started to stir anger inside of me. I tried to cover up my anger by being the class clown, always trying to get people to laugh or fighting just to prove something. But really, the class-clown act was a mask. I was just trying to hide the fact that I didn't feel like I fit in.

At 12 years old, the weight of feeling out of place, not fitting in, and constantly comparing myself to others pushed me into a deep depression. I reached a point where I didn't want to live anymore. One day, I wrote my parents a letter, explaining that the way I felt wasn't their fault but that I couldn't go on. I remember sitting in my room, holding a knife to my throat, ready to end my life. Tears streamed down my face. I reached my breaking point. Then, I heard my mom call out from the kitchen.

"Junior!" she shouted, a nickname my family gave me for being named after my father.

I heard the creaking of the floorboards as Mom walked through the living room toward my bedroom. In a panic, I threw my knife under the bed and wiped my face. She came into my room and saw me crying, not knowing how close she came to losing me that day. Mom hugged me as I told her some lie to escape the truth about why I was in tears. When she left the room, I ripped the goodbye letter out of my composition notebook, tore it into small pieces, and threw it away. I didn't tell her until years later, in 2022, when I made a motivational video explaining how her love unknowingly saved my life.

But my struggles didn't stop there.

By high school, the pressure of trying to fit in and find my way grew stronger. That's when I decided to sign a six-year contract with the Air Force during my senior year of high school. I thought I had found a way out. I'd receive automatic E-2 status once I started basic training *(E-1 is basic airmen status and came with a four-year contract; however, if you sign for an extra two years, you automatically come in at a higher rank than most)*. It felt like the perfect plan, a way for me to secure some sort of structure. I would have a job, money in my pocket, and a way for someone to pay for my education. But not long after signing that contract, I was arrested for robbery. I had just turned 18, and I was being charged as an adult. I was bound to get caught one way or another because that wasn't my first arrest. I had been fighting, trespassing, and committing other minor charges, but this was a major crime, and that arrest changed everything.

I thought my life was over.

I figured a life of prison was in the cards, and maybe becoming a prisoner was who I was destined to be, or at least that's what I convinced myself. I knew that if I went to prison, I'd become the person I was already heading toward—the wrong version of myself.

The witnesses arrived at my lineup, people who saw my face clear as day during the robbery. Needless to say, I was identified and immediately taken to jail, where I remained for three months until my court date. Following my arrest, the Air Force kicked me out before I could begin basic training.

That's when I turned to God in a way that I hadn't in the past. No more surface-level prayers or not knowing God for myself.

"If you get me out of this, I'll serve You. I'll change," I prayed, pleading to Him to bestow mercy on me.

And by His grace, I beat the case. Walking out of that courtroom, free, and heading back to my parents' house was a feeling I'll never forget. It was like all the excuses I had been making, and all the ways I was hiding behind anger and pain came to a full stop. I knew God had given me another shot, and I didn't intend to waste it.

REGGIE WALKER: TAKING OFF THE MASK

After beating the case, I went back to high school. I had a tough road ahead because I had a short window to turn in the assignments that I missed from the prior three months I spent in jail. Thankfully, Mr. Deveaux helped me navigate this mess, and I was able to finish on time. The time I once spent in the disciplinary offices helped me form this relationship with Mr. Deveaux, and with his guidance, I applied to 20 colleges and earned a partial scholarship.

I took this opportunity and ran with it, choosing to attend Georgian Court University in New Jersey. But the thing about college was that I wasn't there to learn; I was there to escape. Growing up in the hood, I knew I needed to get away, and college was my way out. I joined the Educational Opportunity Fund (EOF) program to receive financial support, and that's where I met Reggie Walker, one of the biggest influences in my life.

For those who don't know what an OG is, let me break it down. OG stands for "Original Gangster," but it doesn't necessarily mean they have to be a gangster. In the hood, an OG could be someone older than you who's been through some things and who you respect. Reggie, a man about 16 years older than me, was one of my OGs. He came into the EOF program and gave a talk to the men about "taking off your mask." He broke it down: "We all hide behind this mask we wear, pretending to be tough or something we're not to get through life."

He hit us hard with that message.

Everybody in that room was in tears by the end of his speech because we knew we had been hiding.

Reggie saw right through me. He saw my anger issues and how hard I was trying to be accepted, and from that day forward, he took me under his wing. If you think I'm brutally honest, you will probably fear Reggie. He doesn't sugarcoat anything, and he doesn't let me off the hook for anything, either. He made me face the real me, and that was a turning point for me far before I started training other students.

THE RISE OF "NO EXCUSE"

College brought me back to my roots—boxing. My dad and uncle, who both boxed in Newark, introduced me to the sport when I was seven. Boxing taught me discipline in a way nothing else could, and even though I left it behind in high school to play baseball, I never forgot it. When I got to college, I started boxing again, and that's when things started to click for me.

In 2017, I decided to start posting my workouts on Snapchat. Every morning, around 6 a.m., I'd be in the gym, grinding and posting videos, challenging people with, "I'm here working out, so what's your excuse?" It wasn't about bragging but about holding myself accountable and pushing others to do the same. After doing this every day for an entire semester, people started calling me "No Excuse." That name stuck because it was far more than a name or message; it was the way I lived.

Promoting "No Excuse" didn't stop at Snapchat. Soon, students on campus were coming up to me, asking for advice, wanting to know how I stayed so disciplined. What started as a personal journey turned into something bigger. That summer, the university gave me a job mentoring freshmen, offering me housing in exchange for guiding new students. That's when motivational speaking entered the picture, even though I didn't fully realize this opportunity in the making at the time.

But here's the thing: I'm an athlete. Being an athlete means performing at a high level, and I'm competitive by nature. So, if I'm out here giving advice, I knew I had to keep evolving, too. The "No Excuse" lifestyle wasn't just for show. This was my way of holding myself accountable to be the best version of myself.

Looking back—growing up with struggles, almost ending my life at 12, signing a military contract only to get kicked out after being arrested, facing prison, and finding my way in college—those experiences taught me one priceless lesson: You can't live life stuck in excuses. At some point, you have to face the truth and step into who you're meant to be. I wasn't just fighting for myself but to honor the potential that God gave me.

We are all made in God's image (Genesis 1:27), and that means there's greatness in each of us. But when you make excuses, you reject that greatness. It's like telling God, "I'm not ready to live up to what You've given me." I had to learn the hard way that making excuses isn't just about letting yourself down but about turning your back on the opportunities God has laid out for you. That's why I had to shift my mindset from complaining to executing.

When I stopped making excuses, everything started to align. The moment I chose to honor God by stepping into my potential, I saw how much more I could achieve. Every challenge you face is your chance to prove that you're walking in His greatness. Walking in greatness and the transformation of your mindset from complaining to executing exists in how you carry yourself, how you bounce back, and how you handle life's tests that show what you're made of and who God made You to be.

PART II: SELF-SABOTAGE THROUGH EXCUSES

Excuses are slick. They creep up on you, disguised as reasons why you can't move forward. They make you feel like you're protecting yourself, like they're keeping you safe from failure or embarrassment. But the truth is, excuses are your #1 enemy. They aren't keeping you safe; they're keeping you stuck. If you let them run your life, you'll live in a prison of self-sabotage. And I'm speaking from experience.

Excuses are dangerous because they don't always look like excuses. Sometimes, they seem like valid reasons. You convince yourself you're "too busy," or it's "not the right time." You tell yourself, "I don't have enough resources," or "Once I get X, then I'll start Y." These excuses feel legitimate, but all they do is keep you from taking action. They trap you in the same cycle, making it easy to avoid hard work and risks.

Self-sabotage can be subtle. You might not realize you're doing it. Self-sabotage can look like procrastination, putting off decisions that could push you forward. It can show up as distractions, so instead of focusing on your goals, you're getting lost in things that don't matter. Other times, self-sabotage is loud. It's the frustration that turns into anger, reckless choices, or bad decisions made in moments of confusion, desperation, and self-defeat.

People are quick to blame their circumstances, environment, and past. How many times have you told yourself, "It's not my fault"? How often do you hear, "If only I had X, I'd be successful"?

That's self-sabotage in disguise, and it's dangerous.

The more you tell yourself why you can't do something, the further you get from where you want to be. You end up building excuses instead of building your future.

For years, I was caught in that trap. I convinced myself that my setbacks were because of my circumstances, lack of resources, and others being in a better position. In reality, the real problem was within. My doubts, insecurities, and anger were fueling my excuses. And those excuses kept me exactly where I didn't want to be – stagnant.

TRAPPED IN THE COMFORT ZONE

Comfort zones feel good. They make you feel secure because they're familiar, like you have everything under control. But here's the truth: Comfort zones are a trap. They keep you stuck. I was stuck in that exact place when I was training in New Jersey.

Back in New Jersey, I had built a solid reputation. Really, the man I became was a 180 from my high school years. I drew in countless people because of my personal transformation. Some clients knew me from my days in the streets, but they honored my vulnerability and wisdom. I was now a positive influence from the hood, making legal money, and training reputable professionals, which gave hope to others. I had clients, I was making good money, and I was starting to get noticed, especially on social media, where I was regarded as a top trainer in Jersey. On paper, my life looked great. I had a routine and a packed schedule, and I was comfortable. But then, an opportunity presented itself for me to move to Orlando and train a professional NBA athlete, Cole Anthony, from the Orlando Magic.

Let me be clear—this was a huge opportunity. But with every opportunity comes risk. Taking that chance meant leaving behind everything I had built in Jersey, starting over in a new city where no one knew my name, and having to rebuild my client base from scratch.

The thought of starting over was scary.

You see, comfort zones make you second-guess yourself. They make you think, "Why risk it when things are good here?"

The easy choice would've been to stay in Jersey, where I was already making money and building a name. But here's the thing: Staying in my comfort zone would've kept me in a position of playing small. I knew deep down that staying comfortable wasn't going to get me to the next level of training pro athletes, high-profile professionals, and other like-minded individuals.

In May 2022, I decided to pack up and move to Orlando, but that decision didn't come easy. There were nights when I questioned if I was making the right move. I wondered if leaving behind my clients and starting fresh was the right call. But if you want to grow, you have to get uncomfortable and take risks, and sometimes, those risks mean starting over.

Starting from scratch in Orlando wasn't a walk in the park. There were days when I had to hustle harder than I ever did in Jersey. But the discomfort was worth it. That leap of faith paid off in ways I never imagined. Now, I'm living a better life, working with top-tier athletes and celebrities, and building something far bigger than I could've ever done had I stayed comfortable in Jersey. And that's what people don't realize—comfort zones seem safe, but they limit your growth. You can't reach new levels if you're always playing it safe.

Here's the bottom line: Staying comfortable will keep you stuck, kill your potential, and make you settle for a life that's less than what you deserve. To get where you want to go, you've got to step out of your comfort zone, take risks, face the fear of the unknown, and push through.

FACING THE MIRROR

Most people don't want to face the truth. It's easier to point fingers at circumstances, the past, or other people. But here's the thing: The biggest enemy isn't in the streets, around the corner, or in your office building—it's in the mirror. Self-sabotage comes from within, and it's fueled by the lies we tell ourselves. If you're not willing to look yourself in the eye and be brutally honest, you'll never break free from self-sabotage.

I had that me vs. me moment, standing in front of the mirror, acknowledging how many excuses I had made for why I wasn't where I wanted to be. But really, I was the one holding myself back. No one else was stopping me from making moves, my excuses were.

No one wants to admit that they're the reason they're stuck. But until you do, nothing changes. If you don't call yourself out on your own self-sabotaging ways, you'll stay stuck. Once you see the pattern, you can start tearing it down. And believe me, that's not an easy process. Tearing down your old ways means admitting your fears, doubts, and everything you've been avoiding.

Fear plays a major role in self-sabotage. Most people don't realize how much their fear controls them. It's not just the fear of failure but the fear of success, too. Sometimes, the fear of stepping into your full potential is just as powerful as the fear of falling short. But here's the brutal truth: Fear only has power if you let it. The more you run from fear, the more your fears take ownership over you. But once you face your fears and stand your ground, fear loses its grip.

Facing the mirror is about confronting the truth, being brutally honest with yourself, calling yourself out on your own BS, and deciding that you're done letting excuses run your life. That's the moment things start to change—when you stop hiding behind excuses and start owning your decisions.

SELF-SABOTAGE IN BOXING

Boxing is a perfect example of how self-sabotage can show up. There were times in my boxing career when I skipped workouts, took it easy in the gym, and slacked off on training. And I had every excuse lined up—too tired, too busy, and didn't have the time to put in extra effort.

But the truth?

I was scared of pushing myself too hard and not measuring up to the other fighters.

Excuses let you off the hook, but in the ring, there's no room for excuses. Every time I didn't give 100% in my training, it showed. I'd step into the ring, knowing I wasn't fully prepared, and that self-sabotage showed up in every punch. I wasn't just fighting my opponent; I was fighting my doubts, fears, and insecurities, and it cost me.

Self-sabotage in boxing wasn't just about physical work but mental work, too. Fear controlled me, made me hold back, and led me to believe that if I didn't give it my all, I wouldn't have to deal with the disappointment of losing. But here's the thing: You can't let fear run the show. If you're afraid to give your goals everything you've got because you're scared of failure, you're already losing. The only way to overcome self-sabotage is to stop letting fear dictate your actions.

Once I stopped making excuses and started putting in work, circumstances changed. I wasn't holding back anymore. I faced the fear of not measuring up, and I decided to push through anyway. That's when I started to see progress, not just in the ring, but in my mindset. That's what many people don't understand—self-sabotage is rooted in fear, and fear only has power if you give it permission to run your life.

SELF-SABOTAGE AS A COACH

I didn't only self-sabotage in the ring. Self-sabotage followed me when I transitioned to coaching. When I started coaching, I doubted myself. I questioned whether I had what it took to train other people. Even though I knew I had the skills, fear crept in. I worried about what others would think, and I held back from fully putting myself out there. I waited, thinking clients would come to me because of my skills. That was another excuse. I waited for opportunities to come to me instead of going out and making things happen. I was scared of rejection, afraid that if I put myself out there and didn't succeed, I would be seen as a failure. But here's the thing: Rejection is a part of the process. You'll undoubtedly experience it, but you can't let the fear of rejection stop you from making moves.

When I finally stopped hiding behind my excuses and started going after what I wanted, life shifted. My clientele grew dramatically. I started training actors, influencers, and multiple athletes. Established, successful businesspeople were seeking my opinion on mindset and discipline. What started as a business in my backyard, making $40 per training session, climbed to a six-figure training company. I put myself out there, took risks, and worked through fear. That's when I started to see real progress, not just in my business, but in my mindset. The shift happened when I stopped letting self-sabotage run the show and started executing on what I knew I could do.

BRUTAL TRUTH: EXCUSES ARE KILLING YOUR POTENTIAL

Every time you make an excuse, you choose comfort over growth. You choose to stay small instead of stepping into the greatness that you're capable of. And don't forget that nobody cares about your excuses. Life moves on whether you step up or not.

You've got two choices—let excuses run your life or take control. Because at the end of the day, no one's going to feel sorry for you if you don't make it. The world doesn't owe you anything. It's up to you to stop making excuses and sabotaging yourself and start executing.

I'm not just talking to you; I'm talking to myself, too. I let fear hold me back. I didn't go after certain goals because I was scared of looking dumb or failing. I made excuses like, "It's not the right time," or "I don't have everything figured out yet." And the worst part? The regret of not trying hit me harder than failure ever could. Regret haunted me. These days, when fear shows up, my response is simple: DO IT SCARED. I'd rather try and fail than sit with the heavy feeling of regret.

HOW TO RECOGNIZE AND AVOID SELF-SABOTAGE

Self-sabotage is sneaky, so you need to be honest with yourself and call it out when it happens. Here's how to fight back when fear tries to take over:

1. **Do it scared. Fear ain't the boss**: Fear will always be there. It doesn't magically disappear once you're successful or more confident. Fear is always lurking. But here's the thing—you can't let fear control your life. I had to tell myself, "Randy, you've felt fear before, and you're still here. You've survived every scary moment. You'll survive this, too." So, when fear shows up, don't wait for it to leave. Move forward as it tags along and show it who's boss.
2. **Regret hurts more than fear**: Do you know what's worse than fear? Regret. I've felt both, but I promise that regret is the heaviest burden to carry. I've had those moments where I looked back and thought, "Man, I should've gone harder," or "I wish I just tried." That's a pain I never want to feel again. I understand some regrets are inevitable but for the decisions you can control, you must take advantage of them. Now, I do it scared because I know I'd rather face a setback than sit with the weight of wondering, "What if?"
3. **Break it down. Small wins stack up**: You don't have to conquer fear all at once. You don't need to sprint through the finish line

today. Sometimes, it's about showing up and doing one small thing, then another, and another. Small wins add up over time, and before you know it, you've built momentum. One of the biggest mistakes people make is thinking they need to do something grand right out of the gate. Nah, just show up consistently, no matter how small the action feels. Consistency is where magic happens.

4. **Check your circle. Get around real ones**: This is crucial. You need people who won't let you sit in your excuses, people who will call you out when you're self-sabotaging. My boys do that for me. They don't sugarcoat anything. They'll hit me with, "Bro, stop playing. You said you were going to do this. What happened?" That type of accountability keeps me going. When you have people who see your potential and won't let you settle, you're less likely to fall into the trap of self-sabotage.

A FINAL WORD ON FEAR AND SELF-SABOTAGE

Understand that fear will show up. That's a fact. But what you do when fear shows up is what matters. You can let it control you, or you can choose to push forward. Life will always test you to see how badly you really want it. I know pushing past fear is hard. I've been in those moments where fear felt paralyzing and self-doubt crept in. I wanted to quit, but I didn't, and neither should you. Cut the excuses. Stop self-sabotaging. Take that step, even if it's small. Take it scared. Because when you look back one day, you won't remember your fear, only the courage you showed to push through.

PART III: NO ONE CARES ABOUT YOUR EXCUSES

I need to reiterate this point: No one cares about your excuses or why you couldn't make it happen. The world won't stop and feel sorry for you because things didn't go your way. Life moves on, whether you show up or not. The only thing that matters is whether you did the work and executed what needed to be done. That's the bottom line.

Excuses don't reap results. They don't put food on the table, propel you closer to your goals, or earn respect. You can have all the reasons in the world for why you didn't get it done, but at the end of the day, excuses don't matter. Life is unforgiving in that way. The harsh reality is that nobody will give you a free pass just because you had a tough break. Everybody has ups and downs. No one is immune to struggle. It doesn't matter whether you come from the bottom or top; everyone faces moments when life hits hard. But what separates the people who succeed from the ones who don't is their response to tough breaks. You choose to make excuses, or you choose to execute. It's that simple.

People respect results, not reasons. Have you ever noticed how the people who made it don't spend time talking about why they could've failed? It's because no one cares about the "could've" and "should've" stories. It's about what you did with what you had. You can be a victim of your circumstances, or you can be the person who finds a way to overcome them. And that's a choice only you can make.

PEOPLE HAVE THEIR OWN PROBLEMS

Here's another truth nobody talks about enough: People are dealing with their own lives and problems. This isn't negative or selfish, it's just reality. We're all human beings living life, trying to figure things out, dealing with our own battles. So while you're sitting there, stuck in excuses, thinking the world should stop and help you out, understand that other people are busy living their lives, too.

This is *your* life. No one else is going to live it for you, and no one else will carry your burdens. Blaming others for your circumstances is a waste of energy. Nobody owes you anything. Trust that I'm not being harsh. Instead, I'm telling you the truth so you don't waste your time expecting help that may never come. It would be a shame to waste this beautiful life and even more of a shame to waste the potential of the beautiful life you could build if you just stop making excuses and start owning your actions.

THE WORLD DOESN'T OWE YOU ANYTHING

There's a saying that "life is 10% what happens to you and 90% how you respond to it." That couldn't be truer. It's not about the hand you're dealt. It's about how you play it. Plenty of people come from tough backgrounds, but they decide to rise above it. That's the difference between winners and everyone else.

When I was younger, I used to think that because I was struggling and didn't have what other kids had that people would give me a break. I thought people would see that I didn't have the same opportunities and feel sorry for me. But that never happened. No one gave me a break, and I had to learn the hard way that no one would do the work for me. The world doesn't care about your excuses, background, or circumstances. You figure it out, or you don't.

FOR THE ONES THAT THINK THEY'RE TOO LATE

I don't care how old you are. I don't care how long you've been sitting there telling yourself it's too late. I don't care if you've spent ten, 20, or 30 years thinking, "My time passed, I missed my window." It's not too late. You can start today. Right now. People love to say, "I'm too far behind," or "I missed my chance."

No, you didn't.

That's just another excuse you're hiding behind.

Life doesn't care how old you are. Life only cares if you're ready to move. Every day you wait is a day you'll never get back. Don't let the fear of starting late keep you from starting at all.

Let me hit you with something real: Progress doesn't have an age limit, and success doesn't have a deadline. If you think you're too late, just look at how many people started "late" and still made something out of their lives. Colonel Sanders didn't start KFC until he was in his 60s. Samuel L. Jackson didn't become a household name until he was in his 40s. Everybody loves Oprah Winfrey, right? Well, she was fired from her first TV job and didn't hit her stride until her 30s. One of my favorite motivators, Steve Harvey, was once homeless, living in his car, before making it big. Those people could've said, "It's too late," but they didn't. They started anyway.

I'll keep it 100 with you. The best time to start was yesterday. But since we can't change that, the second-best time to start is now. Don't let another day go by where you sit in regret, thinking about what could've been. That kind of thinking gets you nowhere.

Look, I've been there. I've wasted time. I've let fear and doubt control my moves. I've sat around waiting for the perfect time, thinking that if I just waited long enough, the stars would align, and everything would feel right.

And guess what happened?

Nothing.

Nothing happened until I decided to move, even when it didn't feel right. And every time I waited too long, the regret hit me harder than the fear of failing ever could.

Every day you wait, someone else is out there grinding, making moves, and inching closer to their goals. But this isn't about competing with them. It's about competing with yourself. It's about deciding that you're done waiting and ready to start, no matter how far behind you think you are.

You don't need to have everything figured out. Just take the first step. This first step doesn't have to be big or perfect. It just has to be done. Set a small goal. Make a small move. Do something. That first step might seem insignificant, but it's the beginning of something bigger.

If you've been waiting for a sign, this is it. This is your moment. Stop thinking you need a perfect time or perfect opportunity. The perfect time is when you decide to move. And if that's right now, get up and make it happen.

I know starting late feels hard. You might be thinking that you'll never catch up, but it's better to start late than to never start at all. Time will pass either way. Whether you start now or sit around waiting, five years from now will come. The only difference is, if you start today, five years from now, you'll be five years into progress. Think about that. Five years from now, you can remain stuck in the same spot or five years closer to everything you want. The choice is yours.

You've learned about my story and that I didn't always get it right. I made a lot of mistakes, I wasted time, and I let fear and doubt keep me from moving. But at some point, I made a choice. I chose to stop waiting and to start building, even when I felt like it was too late. And because of that decision, I'm here today, sharing this message with you. If a kid from East Orange, who went from making dumb mistakes to building a brand and inspiring others, can start late and still make it work, so can you.

This is your fresh start. Right here. Right now. I don't care if you're 20, 40, or 60—start where you are. Use what you have. Do what you can. Don't waste any more time thinking about what could've been. Focus on what can be. Stop living in the past. The past does not define you, but the moves you make today do. You've got this. I believe in you. Now is the time for you to believe in yourself. No excuses.

EXECUTION IS ALL THAT MATTERS

At the end of the day, execution counts. The world rewards people who get things done, not the ones with the best excuses. It doesn't matter how talented you are, how much potential you have, or how many good ideas are in your head. None of that matters if you don't execute.

Think about the people who inspire you, the ones out there killing it in their field. Do you think they got there by making excuses?

No.

They got there by executing, by doing the work every day, even when it was hard. They didn't wait for the right conditions or hope for a lucky break. They made it happen. They showed up every day and did the work. That's what sets them apart.

And this isn't just about reaching your goals. It's about the mindset you build and sustain along the way. Execution breeds discipline. Execution forces you to push through challenges, problem-solve, and persevere when plans don't go your way. Every time you choose execution over excuses, you grow stronger. You start to trust yourself more, knowing that no matter what life throws at you, you'll find a way to figure it out. That's what builds real confidence.

BRUTAL TRUTH: RESULTS OVER EXCUSES

Here's another unfiltered truth: Results are all that matter. No one cares about your reasons, no one cares about the obstacles you have to face, and no one cares about your excuses. The only thing that people will remember is whether you delivered. You can have all the potential in the world, but potential doesn't count if you don't execute.

Life is like a card game. You're dealt a hand of cards, and you have no control over which cards you receive. You could get a terrible hand or a great hand, but here's the thing: You can lose with the best hand,

and you can still win with the worst. It's not about the cards themselves but about how you play them. Your strategy, mindset, and adaptability are what matter. Skills and determination will set you apart. When you look back on your life, do you want to be the person who talks about what could've been, or do you want to be the person who made things happen? That's the real question.

Results will define you, not your struggles. So stop holding on to your excuses and waiting for the perfect moment and start executing. The only thing standing between you and your goals is the work you haven't done yet. No one's coming to save you. No one's going to hand you success. You have to go out there, take control of your life, and make it happen. Because at the end of the day, the only thing that counts is execution.

PART IV: WHAT EXECUTION REALLY LOOKS LIKE

Execution isn't some feel-good idea. It's about grinding it out, day in and day out, no matter how you feel or what's going on. Execution is about doing the work, whether you're in the mood or not. And let's be real—most days, you won't be in the mood.

Too many people think they know what execution means. They think it's about having a plan, talking about their goals, or hyping themselves up on Monday mornings. But that's not execution. Execution is about action, moving forward when you don't have all the answers, and taking the next step, even when the path looks blurry. It's being willing to fail, adjust, and keep pushing forward.

Execution is waking up when you're tired. It's hitting the gym when your body aches. It's putting in the work when everyone else is taking it easy. Execution doesn't care how you feel; it only cares that you show up. It's not flashy or exciting, and most of the time, it's uncomfortable. But execution is the only way to get from where you are to where you want to be.

THE POWER OF SMALL, CONSISTENT ACTIONS

People think execution is about big moves and breakthroughs. They think execution is about massive changes happening all at once. But real execution is in the small, daily actions that add up over time. It's the little things—getting up early, making that extra phone call, reading a few pages when you'd rather watch TV—that move the needle forward.

Execution is like building a brick wall. You don't throw the whole wall up in a day. You lay one brick at a time, and eventually, the wall takes shape. Nipsey Hussle said it best: "The game is gonna test you. Never fold. Stay ten toes down. It's not on you, it's in you. And what's in you, they can't take away." His whole philosophy was about slow, steady progress, laying down bricks every day until the wall is built. And that's the same mindset you need to develop.

The grind is personal, and I don't take my journey lightly. That's the same approach I took when my best friend, Bryce Council, and I started the #3B47 movement. #3B47 stands for "3 Wins Before 7AM." But for us, time isn't the most important part; it's about getting those three wins in before facing the world. It's about setting the tone for your day by winning the morning. Those three wins could be an early morning workout, reading something to feed your mind, or finishing a task that pushes you forward. The point is, before the world hits you with distractions, stress, and demands, you've already locked in three wins for yourself. The power of #3B47 is that it gives you control over your day. You're not waiting for things to happen; you're starting strong and stacking wins from the moment you wake up. #3B47 is a movement built on the idea that no matter how big your goals are, they start with small, daily wins. If you can get three wins in before the world wakes up, the rest of the day is yours. And that's the mindset we wanted to create with #3B47. Every day is an opportunity to lay bricks—small, consistent actions that lead to something massive. #3B47 isn't just something I created with my best friend; it's a movement that anyone can join.

You don't need money.

You don't need special skills.

You don't need permission.

All you need is the discipline to commit to winning your mornings.

So, ask yourself which three things you can do every morning to set yourself up for success.

How are you starting your day, and is it helping you build momentum or keeping you stagnant?

If you had already been stacking daily wins for the past six months, where would you be today?

What excuses are you making for not taking control of each morning?

Are you willing to challenge yourself for the next 30 days to commit to #3B47 and see what happens?

The same way I laid my foundation, brick by brick, is the same way you will build for your future. Start tomorrow. Start today. Start now. Because if you can get those first three wins before the world wakes up, the rest of the day is yours.

EXECUTION AS WORSHIP TO GOD

There's another level to execution that's deeper than achieving goals and success. It's about honoring God. Something that me and my client (and pastor) Tye Tribbett talk about is how execution is a form of worship. Tye always says, "Execution is how you show God you value the gifts He gave you."

Think about that.

Every time you take action, work hard, and push toward something meaningful, you're honoring the Creator who gave you those abilities in the first place. God didn't bless us with talents and purpose just for us to sit on them. Execution is how we show appreciation and honor His blessings. Action is a form of spiritual discipline. When you execute, you're working for something much bigger than yourself.

So, when you're laying those bricks every day, whether in your job, in your personal goals, or in your fitness—understand that this isn't just about you. Execution and small, consistent steps are about honoring God, using the gifts He gave you, and showing up, day after day, as a way of worship. That's a perspective shift that changes everything. Grinding is not just about success. It's about living in a way that honors the purpose you've been given.

NO ROOM FOR PERFECTION

Here's another misconception people have about execution: Everything has to be perfect before they can move. They wait for the right time, the right plan, and the right circumstances. But that's just another excuse. Perfection is a lie. It doesn't exist.

If you're sitting around waiting for the perfect moment to take action, you're already losing. Execution is about getting started right where you are with what you've got. It's about taking messy, imperfect action and figuring things out as you go. You can't wait for everything to be perfectly lined up because it never will be. Life doesn't work like that. Execution is about moving forward, even when you don't have all the answers. It's about starting with the resources you have and making adjustments along the way. The people who wait for everything to be perfect end up stuck. The ones who execute, even when circumstances aren't ideal, are the ones who make progress.

Perfection is the enemy of execution. If you want to get things done, you must let go of the idea that everything needs to be flawless. Instead, focus on moving the ball forward. You can fix mistakes along the way, but you can't fix inaction.

WHAT EXECUTION FEELS LIKE

Execution doesn't feel good. There's nothing glamorous about execution. It's not a motivational Instagram post. It's not a highlight reel. Execution is what happens behind the scenes when no one's watching, and it's ugly. It's pushing through when your body's screaming for rest. It's staying up late to finish a project no one's going to give you credit for. It's putting in the work when you're frustrated, tired, and questioning whether it's worth it.

Most people think they need to "feel motivated" to execute. But motivation is a temporary feeling. It comes and goes. Execution doesn't care about your feelings; it cares about your discipline. It's about showing up, day after day, especially when you don't feel like it.

The real test of execution is whether you can keep grinding when the excitement is gone. Everyone loves starting a new project, setting a new goal, and feeling that initial rush of excitement. But what happens when that excitement fades? That's when most people quit. They lose motivation, and they think it's a sign to stop. But that's where execution separates the winners from the rest.

Execution feels like putting in the work when you're not seeing results right away. It feels like pushing through doubt, frustration, and boredom. Execution is not always fun, but it's necessary. The real work happens in those moments when you feel like giving up but choose to keep going.

HOW TO START EXECUTING TODAY

If you want to start executing, don't overthink it, just act. People waste too much time planning, thinking, and waiting for the perfect moment. The truth is you don't need a perfect plan to start. You just need to take the first step. Here's how you can start executing today:

1. **Do one thing right now.** Whatever goal you have, break it down into small actions and do one immediately. Don't wait until tomorrow or next week—act today. Your first step doesn't have to be big. It just has to be something that moves you forward.
2. **Stop waiting for the "perfect" time.** There's no such thing. Life won't line up perfectly for you to chase your goals. Stop using perfection as an excuse and start with what you have. If you're always waiting for the right time, you'll be stuck forever.
3. **Be relentless.** Execution is about consistency. It's not about doing something once and hoping it sticks. It's about showing up every day and doing the work. Relentlessly. If you want to see results, you must be willing to grind every day.
4. **Measure your progress.** Keep track of your actions. Whether you use a notebook or an app, track your work. Seeing progress, even in small doses, motivates you to keep going.

EXECUTION OVER EXCITEMENT

Let's get real. Execution will always beat excitement. Everyone starts out excited. Everyone loves to talk about their goals, dreams, and big plans, but excitement fades. The real question is, what are you going to do when the hype wears off and the grind sets in? Because that's when the ability to execute matters most. Once the initial rush is gone, most people fold. They fall back on excuses, telling themselves they'll get back to it later. But the winners?

They execute when they're not excited.

They execute when they're tired.

They execute when they're unmotivated.

They execute when life isn't going their way.

They don't rely on excitement to keep going; they rely on discipline. If you want to win, you must let go of the need to feel excited all the time. Execution isn't about how you feel in the moment. Execution is about showing up, doing the work, and trusting that the results will come if you stay consistent. Stop chasing excitement and start committing to execution. That's the only way to get where you want to go.

PART V: EMBRACING THE GRIND

Success doesn't come from comfort or from the times when everything is going smoothly. Success is built in the grind. It's the tough days, long hours, and moments when you want to quit but keep pushing anyway.

Most people look at the grind as something to avoid or something to get through so they can enjoy success on the other side. But if you really want to succeed, you have to flip that mindset. The grind isn't something to be avoided. It's something to be embraced. The grind is where you grow and become stronger, more disciplined, and more resilient.

You have to learn to love the process, even when it's uncomfortable. Especially when it's uncomfortable. Because the grind is the only way to get where you want to go. There's no shortcut and no easy way around it. The grind is the path to success.

THE PAIN OF GROWTH

Let's get real. Growth is painful and uncomfortable. And growth isn't always fun. Everyone talks about wanting to grow, but when they realize that growth requires discomfort, they start looking for the exit. But here's a brutal truth: If you're not willing to get uncomfortable, you're not going to grow.

You must accept that pain is part of the process. When you push yourself beyond your limits, whether in the gym, in your business, or in your personal development, it will hurt. It's supposed to hurt. That's how you know you're making progress. If it were easy, everybody would be doing it.

Think about muscles. When you work out, you're tearing muscle fibers. This process hurts and burns, and you'll probably feel like quitting. But those tears are necessary for the muscle to grow stronger.

The same applies to every area of your life.

Growth requires tearing down the old version of yourself so the new, stronger version can emerge.

If you avoid pain, you avoid growth.

This is where most people struggle. They want the results, but they don't want the pain that comes with it. They want strength without discomfort. They want success without sacrifice. The problem is you can't have one without the other. You don't grow through the easy days. You grow through the hard ones. You grow when you push yourself beyond what you thought were your limits. And that's where you find out what you're really made of.

Everyone wants growth until they realize it costs something. Growth costs time, energy, and sometimes peace of mind. You'll be stretched and challenged, and you'll want to give up more times than you can count. But here's the thing—the people who grow, the ones who truly elevate, are the ones who embrace that pain. They don't run from it. They lean into it. They understand that discomfort is the price of admission for the life they want to live.

GET COMFORTABLE BEING UNCOMFORTABLE

One of the most important mindset shifts you can make is learning to get comfortable being uncomfortable. This is where most people fail. They start chasing a goal, but as soon as they hit resistance, they quit. They start telling themselves that maybe this isn't for them, that maybe they should wait until things get easier. But here's the truth: The pathway to success never gets easy. You just get stronger.

Kobe Bryant was all about embracing discomfort. Kobe was one of the greatest basketball players to ever play the game. Known for his relentless work ethic and what he called the "Mamba Mentality," he was all about pushing through pain and discomfort to reach greatness. He said, "Everything negative – pressure, challenges – is all an opportunity for me to rise." Kobe wasn't just talking about physical challenges but mental challenges, too. He knew that the discomfort, grind, and struggle were all part of the journey. Leaning into discomfort separates great from good. Kobe loved the grind because he knew it was making him better. And if you want to reach that next level, you've got to adopt that same mindset.

MY MORNING ROUTINE: THE POWER OF THREE WINS

People always think it's easy for me to wake up early and grind. They see me up at 4 am, getting it done, and assume it's second nature. But let me be real. This level of commitment is not easy to maintain. I'm human. I like to sleep, too. But I know my why. I know my purpose, and I know what I'm after – to help people break free from limitations holding them back and that have held me back for years. My why is to make my father proud and lift up his name while he's in Heaven rejoicing. My why is to take care of my mom and sister and to fill in where my father left behind. My why is to prove to myself that every tear, every courageous decision I made not to commit suicide, every sleepless night, and every night I picked myself backup after failing was all worth it and that I am who I say I am. I was born not only to survive but to prosper, to be a leader, to share value all around the world, to be an inspiration, to be God's servant. My purpose is to push people to see their potential, to challenge them to stop making excuses, and to help them transform their lives through discipline, resilience, and brutal honesty. My purpose is to help people walk in the greatest version of themselves, so I have to suck it up and do what I need to do.

Before I step into the world and give advice, train clients, or motivate others, I have to make sure I'm okay first. So, I get my three wins in before I interact with others. You can't help others if you're not right within. Whether it's getting a workout in, reading something that feeds my mind, or working on a task that pushes me forward, those three wins set the tone for my day. They're my foundation. It's not about being perfect. It's about being prepared. And those three wins? They prepare me to face the world and give it my best every day.

TRAINING IN MY BACKYARD: THE NOEXCUSE FACTORY

After college, I began training clients in my backyard while living in an unfinished basement. I didn't have a lot, just a $40 tent, some rusty dumbbells, and whatever equipment I could afford. The conditions were rough, but I didn't let that stop me. Charging people to train in my backyard wasn't easy. The rain made the ground muddy, and insects were everywhere. It wasn't glamorous at all. I started with three clients. Three grew to ten, and before I knew it, my backyard was crowded. So, I expanded to accept online clients.

Despite my rundown backyard "gym," I made damn sure people knew the results I was delivering. I was pushing my transformations and workouts heavy on social media—posting every day, showing the grind, the sweat, the progress. My Snapchat and Instagram were filled with videos of my clients hitting PRs, before-and-after transformations, and putting people through hell (in the best way possible). I wasn't just training people; I was building a movement. And when people saw that, they wanted in. Now, don't get me wrong. Outsiders had a lot to say.

"Why's he charging y'all for backyard training?"

"Bro really got people paying to train outside?"

But the people actually putting in the work? They didn't question it. They showed up, paid their dues, and got results, and I knew my effort would pay off for my clients and for me, too. That's why I called it the NoExcuse Factory because it was a testament to myself—no excuses.

No excuse not to train.

No excuse not to work out.

No excuse not to officially start my career and pursue my dream.

This area symbolized doing whatever it took, no matter the conditions.

I always knew my hard work would pay off, but I was frustrated with how long it seemed to take. The grind is hard when you're standing in the mud after a rainy day, surrounded by rusty dumbbells, trying to get people to believe in your vision. But I kept going because I understood that growth comes through discomfort. I could've waited for better resources or circumstances, but I didn't. I embraced the grind and kept working.

My backyard grind laid the foundation for everything I've built since. It taught me that no matter how tough things get, if you embrace the grind and push through, you can create something amazing.

HOW TO EMBRACE THE GRIND

If you're going to succeed, you have to make peace with the grind. You have to stop seeing the grind as something negative and start seeing it as the pathway to success. Here's how to start embracing the grind:

1. **Change your perspective.** Stop thinking of the grind as something to get through. Start seeing it as an opportunity to grow. Every time you push through discomfort, you're becoming stronger.
2. **Focus on the process.** Instead of obsessing over results, focus on the steps you're taking every day. Set small goals and celebrate the progress you make along the way. The grind is where growth happens, so appreciate the journey.
3. **Show up every day.** The grind isn't glamorous. The grind is about consistency, showing up day after day, and doing the work. Don't rely on motivation. Rely on discipline. Show up when you don't feel like it.
4. **Learn to love the struggle.** The more you embrace the struggle, the easier it becomes to push through. Stop avoiding discomfort. Lean into it. The struggle is where you grow.

THE GRIND IS THE GATEWAY

The grind is the gateway to everything you want in life. Success doesn't happen in comfort zones. It happens in the grind. It happens in the early mornings, the late nights, and the moments when you're tempted to quit but keep going anyway. Everything worth having costs something, whether it's time, money, or energy. If your dreams are big, and I encourage you to dream big, then you'll need to prove how bad you want it. Life puts roadblocks in our way to test us. Those who really want it will go through the roadblocks. Those who just talk will stay at a starting point, mentioning everything in their way instead of facing it.

If you're serious about success, you have to make peace with the grind. You have to understand that there is no easy way around it. The grind is the only way. And the sooner you embrace the grind, the sooner you'll make real progress. The grind is where winners are made and champions are built. If you learn to love the process and embrace discomfort, there's nothing you can't achieve.

PART VI: HONORING YOUR WORD TO YOURSELF

Self-discipline is the glue that holds your goals and commitments together to achieve success. Without discipline, you're playing a losing game. Talent alone isn't enough. I don't care if you're the most gifted person on the planet. Without discipline, your world will crumble the second you're tested.

How many times have we seen athletes rise to the top, only to throw it all away?

They had the skill, talent, and raw ability, but they lacked discipline to maintain it. Talent can make you shine, but discipline keeps you steady when life gets rough.

You can reach high levels based on talent alone. You might even get lucky and land some big wins. But here's the truth: Without discipline, you're a house built on sand. One wave, one storm, and your house falls apart. Discipline keeps you grounded. It's the anchor that holds you steady. You can't buy it, and you can't fake it. Discipline is built one choice at a time, through the moments when you decide to show up and put in the work, even when it's uncomfortable.

I've watched people with incredible talent lose it all because they couldn't control themselves, guys from the hood who had it all—Division-I offers, elite scholarship, and full rides to top schools—but they got caught up in street life and wrapped up in the wrong crowd, and they never made it out. They let their impulses dictate their actions, and they paid the price.

Don't be that person.

Don't let your lack of discipline be the reason you lose everything you've worked for.

Discipline isn't about perfection; it's about resilience and having the strength to do what needs to be done, no matter how you feel. Talent can take you places, but discipline will keep you there.

HONORING YOUR WORD TO YOURSELF

Let's get real about what it means to honor your word. Honoring your word isn't an abstract concept. It's a personal commitment. I haven't always kept my word to myself. There were times I fell short, like in boxing, and it cost me. Not keeping my promises chipped away at my credibility, opportunities, and relationships. I lost count of how many times I said I'd do something and didn't follow through. At first, those unkept promises seemed small, maybe even unimportant, but they added up, and they weighed me down.

I remember failing a religious course in college, simply because I kept postponing assignments. Not because the work was hard, not because I couldn't handle it, but because I let procrastination run the show. I told myself I had time, that I'd do it tomorrow, but tomorrow kept turning into next week, then next month, until it was too late. That one little delay turned into a failing grade, and I had no one to blame but myself.

I did the same thing in my early career. I lost a client before I had the chance to prove myself, all because I didn't follow up when I said I would. They were ready to train, ready to invest in themselves, and all I had to do was show up and be consistent. But I kept postponing our meetings and delaying responses, thinking they'd wait. They didn't, and I paid for it.

But the hardest loss?

I lost the Golden Gloves because of this bad habit. I wasn't outworked or out-skilled. I beat myself. I slacked on training, skipped workouts, and didn't push myself as hard as I knew I could. I let excuses creep in. I told myself I'd go harder tomorrow, but tomorrow never comes for people who operate this way. When fight night came, I wasn't ready, not because I wasn't talented enough, but because I didn't honor my word in the days leading up to it.

That's when it hit me: I was losing because of ME. Not because of lack of opportunity or bad luck, but because I was building a habit of breaking my own word. And once I realized that, I had two choices: Keep living this way and keep losing, or change.

So, I changed.

I stopped making empty promises to myself. If I said I was going to do something, I did it. If I said I was going to train, I trained. If I said I was going to wake up early, I got my butt up. No snooze button. No excuses.

Breaking promises to yourself is the fastest way to lose self-respect. I remember telling myself I'd start new routines, stay disciplined, and make changes, and then I'd fall short. Each time I failed, I could feel my self-respect slipping away. When you don't honor your word, you're sending yourself a message, saying, "My word doesn't matter." If you keep telling yourself that, you'll start to believe it. And when you don't trust your own word, how can anyone else?

Here's another hard truth: Keeping your word to yourself is the foundation of discipline. Every time you keep a promise to yourself, you build strength and confidence. Keeping your word isn't just about getting things done. It's about showing yourself that you're capable, reliable, and trustworthy. And that's where power begins to build in your life.

THE CONSEQUENCES OF LYING TO YOURSELF

Here's a brutal truth: When you break promises to yourself, you're lying to yourself. And lying to yourself is the first step down a path that leads nowhere. I know what it's like to justify failures, make excuses, and tell yourself that you'll "get to it tomorrow." But here's the thing—the more you lie to yourself, the easier lying becomes. Eventually, you won't realize you're doing it because lying has become second nature.

When you get comfortable lying to yourself, you lose faith in your own word. You justify missed opportunities, slack on your goals, and settle for less than you're capable of. It's a slow fade into mediocrity.

The worst part?

You're the one who put yourself there.

When you lie to yourself, you're setting yourself up for a cycle of disappointment, frustration, and regret, all because you couldn't be honest.

The good news is you can break the cycle. But breaking the cycle starts with brutal honesty, looking yourself in the mirror, and calling yourself out. If you want to grow and achieve something real, you've got to start by telling the truth. Success starts with self-respect, and self-respect starts with keeping your word. If you're lying to yourself, you're robbing yourself of the life you could have. It's time to start being real with yourself. Until you do, you'll stay exactly where you are.

DAILY ACTIONS SHAPE YOUR LIFE

My friend, Joshua Johnson, owner of Seana's restaurant, shared a story on my podcast, "Cut The Excuse." Seana's is a family-owned Caribbean-soul food spot in Orlando, one of the most highly rated restaurants at that. Joshua built a relationship with billionaire investor and entrepreneur Mark Cuban just by doing something most people overlook – answering an email on time and handling his business. That might sound small, but here's what happened next. Because Joshua responded immediately and professionally, that move opened doors that most people only dream about. That one email leveraged an opportunity to cater for an entire NBA season.

If you don't remember, during the height of COVID-19, the NBA created a "bubble" in Orlando, where players, coaches, and staff were isolated to safely finish the season. Only a handful of restaurants were given the chance to cater to the league, and Josh's restaurant, Seana's Caribbean Soul Food, made the cut.

His story proves something powerful: You never know which action will change your life, but if you handle your business with urgency and professionalism, opportunities will come. Most people miss out on life-changing moments because they drag their feet. They hesitate. They ignore that email. They say, "I'll get to it later," and by the time they finally respond, the opportunity is gone. This is why execution is everything.

When the opportunity shows up, will you be ready, or will you let it slip because you hesitated?

Joshua's story is a perfect example of how small actions shape your life. Taking action is not about big, flashy moments; it's about the little things you do when no one's watching. The daily habits, routines, and consistency set you apart. Those small, seemingly insignificant choices add up to create the life you want. If you're not handling the small things, you'll never be ready for the big ones. After all, success isn't built on one grand gesture but on the little wins.

Think about the importance of daily action from this perspective—every time you skip a workout, hit snooze, or make an excuse, you're telling yourself that your health doesn't matter. Those small actions create your reality. You might not see the effects right away, but over time, those choices build momentum. They shape your character, mindset, and, ultimately, your life. If you want to reach your goals, start by nailing the basics. Do the small things right, and the big things will take care of themselves.

EMBRACING ROUTINE AND BEING INTENTIONAL WITH TIME

Routine isn't just about structure; it's about respect for your goals, your time, and yourself. I've learned over the years that time is our most valuable resource. You can get more money, more friends, and more opportunities, but once time is gone, it's gone for good. That's why people who understand success charge high prices for their time. They know their worth, and they don't waste it.

Having a routine forces you to be intentional with your time. A routine keeps you focused, grounded, and on track. When you build a routine, you're not leaving life to chance. You're saying, "This is my time, and I'm going to use it wisely." A routine helps you cut distractions, eliminate excuses, and focus on what matters. Establishing a routine is about setting yourself up for daily success.

When you're intentional with your time, you're making a statement. You're telling yourself and the world that you're serious about where you're going. You're proving that you value your life enough to make your time a priority. And when you start respecting your time, other people will, too. They'll see that you're not here to play around but to make things happen. Routine isn't about restriction; it's about freedom to spend your time where it counts and to live a life that aligns with your goals.

BRUTAL TRUTH: YOU ARE WHAT YOU REPEATEDLY DO

In the words of Aristotle, you are what you repeatedly do. It doesn't matter what you say you're going to do but what you actually do. Your life is a reflection of your habits, plain and simple. If you're constantly breaking promises, that's who you are—a person who doesn't keep their word. Excuses are cheap. They're easy to make, easy to believe, and easy to hide behind. But they won't get you anywhere. But if you make it a habit to honor your word, to follow through on your commitments, you become a person of integrity.

HOW TO START HONORING YOUR WORD TO YOURSELF

1. **Start small**. You don't need to go big right away. Pick one promise. Keep it. Then, build from there.
2. **Track your progress**. Write down what you say you're going to do and track your progress (or lack thereof). This will hold you accountable and show you where you need to tighten up.
3. **Stop making excuses**. When you're about to break a promise, stop for a moment. Remember why you made the promise in the first place. Excuses are a trap. Don't fall for them.

4. **Celebrate your wins**. Every time you keep a promise, celebrate. Small wins build confidence and reinforce the habit of discipline.

CHAPTER TWO: UNDERSTANDING YOUR WHY

PART I: THE POWER OF PURPOSE

Purpose is not just a word. It's the reason you push forward when life tries to knock you down. But here's the thing: Purpose doesn't have to be one unchanging path you pursue. Instead, purpose evolves as you evolve. Your purpose changes as you go through different seasons. And let me tell you—purpose is not something you find sitting still.

I got a glimpse of purpose when I left the hood and stepped onto a college campus. I saw people from different backgrounds and realized there was so much more I wanted to experience. I didn't want to be stuck in the cycle of mistakes and going nowhere fast. I knew I was built for more. That's when I realized I had to break out and push for something different.

But it wasn't until I started training others that my purpose took hold of me. When people saw the changes I was making in my life, they wanted in. They'd ask me to coach them and help them get to where I was. That gave me something real to live for. I wasn't just out here for me. Now, I had people counting on me to show them the way. That's when I learned that my journey wasn't just about getting fit but about making an impact. When I started training, it began about me. It was about getting my head right and finding a way to deal with my built-up anger. But as people started to notice, I realized my actions were making an impact. I went from a criminal, someone who could have easily been another statistic, to someone living with purpose. And I didn't have to say a word because people saw it in the way I showed up.

I didn't know my purpose would come from a personal fitness journey, but looking back, I can see how it all lined up. Training wasn't just about getting in shape. It was about proving to myself that I could be something more and showing others that they could do the same. When you live with purpose, people take note, and that's when you start to see that your story isn't just for you. It's for everyone.

When my father passed away unexpectedly in 2020 due to a heart attack, the fire within reignited, especially because my dad was just getting back into fitness. Losing him reminded me that life is short, and I wanted to honor him by building something that would outlast both of us. I wanted to leave a legacy, live with purpose, and leave a mark.

But here's what I want you to know: I know we all hear that you need a "why," but the truth is, you can have a big "why" that pushes you *and* have smaller "whys" that keep you moving each day. Your why isn't set in stone. Your why can change depending on where you're at in life. Some days, I lean on my big "why" of honoring my dad and building a legacy. Other days, my why is simpler—following through to prove to myself that I can. Sometimes, I wake up simply trying to make it through the day without quitting. When I hit a rut, and believe me, I hit them too, I go back to my reason of why I started in the first place, and that's to never be the old version of myself or end up back in the penitentiary. I'll watch old videos of myself training or speaking, something to remind me of how far I've come. Or I'll watch videos of luxury lifestyles, reminding myself of where I'm headed. I feed my brain with "food" that push me to act. Sometimes, it's a sermon. Sometimes, it's a podcast, as long as it helps me get back on track. Purpose is powerful, but you must feed it and keep it alive every day.

So, don't feel like you need some big, grand purpose. Find what moves you today, this week, or this month. Start there and build on it. And when you find that purpose, protect it, feed it, and let it push you through tough times. And when life changes, let your purpose change with you.

Reflection
- **Honesty moment**: Think about a recent time when you felt stuck. What got you back on track? What small "why" pushed you through that moment?
- **Write a letter to your future self:** Take a moment to write a letter to your future self, the person you will be a few years from today. Describe the purpose you're living for and the actions you're taking to stay true to it. Talk about how your purpose will grow and where you want to be a few years from now.

- **Visualize your future:** Find a video or an image that represents the life you want to live. Watch it or look at it daily to remind yourself of what you're working toward. Write down why this vision fuels your purpose.

PART II: FINDING YOUR WHY

Purpose isn't something that just shows up. It's something you discover. Sometimes, your purpose finds you when you least expect it. For me, my purpose started as an escape. I wasn't out here trying to inspire people. I was trying to survive and find some way to deal with the anger building up inside. I started training again, not for anybody else, but because I needed to release rage and work through the mess in my head.

But then something happened.

People saw me go from someone who could have ended up behind bars for good to someone who was turning my life around. They watched me as I transformed from a criminal to an influence.

And that's when it hit me: I had a purpose beyond getting fit but to show others that no matter what you're going through or where you've been, there's no excuse not to keep pushing.

Your purpose might not show up with flashing lights. It might start as something you're doing for yourself, something that helps you make it through the day. Purpose has a way of finding you when you're in the middle of the grind, showing you that your actions can speak louder than any words.

So, how do you find your "why"? You start by looking at what drives you and keeps you going when everything else is falling apart. Here are a few questions that can help you dig a little deeper:

What would I fight for, even if it's hard?

Your purpose isn't always easy. If you're willing to push through the pain for something, that's a sign it matters to you.

How do I want to impact those around me?

Purpose isn't just about you. It's about what you leave behind and those you touch along the way. What kind of influence do you want to have on the world?

What keeps calling me back, even when it would be easier to walk away?

If something keeps coming back around, even when it's tough, that's a sign. Purpose has a way of pulling you in, making it impossible to quit.

You might not know the answer right away. Purpose takes time, and it's okay if your purpose doesn't look like anyone else's. Really, it shouldn't. This is about what drives you, what keeps you up at night, and what gets you out of bed in the morning.

STEP-BY-STEP GUIDE: CLARIFYING YOUR PURPOSE

1. **Look back on your story**. What have you been through that has shaped who you are? Think about moments that have defined you and struggles that made you stronger. Purpose often grows from experiences.

2. **Identify your passions**. What do you care about unwaveringly? What's something you'd do even if no one paid you? Your passions are a window into your purpose.
3. **Define your values**. What do you stand for and what guides your decisions? Identify your core values. Purpose is rooted in beliefs.
4. **Think about the legacy you want to leave**. Picture yourself at the end of your life. What do you want to be remembered for? What impact do you want to make? Your purpose is your chance to shape that legacy.
5. **Try and adjust**. Don't worry about getting it perfect. Purpose isn't always clear-cut. Get started, try things out, and let your purpose grow with you.

Reflection

- **Reflection prompt:** What moment in your life changed you? What did it teach you, and how has that moment shaped who you are today?
- **Define your values:** Write your top five principles you won't compromise. Then, think about how they connect to your purpose. What do they say about what matters most to you?
- **Identify your passions:** List three things you're passionate about, even if they seem small. Now, think about how those passions might fit into a larger purpose. What do they reveal about what drives you?
- **Visualize your legacy:** Picture yourself at the end of your life. What do you want people to remember about you? Write down what you want to have accomplished and the impact you want to have made.

GAINING EXTERNAL PERSPECTIVE

Sometimes, figuring out your purpose requires stepping outside of yourself. This next exercise is something my sister, Clarise, suggested I share because of how powerful it was for her. When she felt stuck, trying to find clarity on her next steps, she did something simple but profound—she reached out to people she trusted and asked for their honest perspective on how they saw her. This exercise wasn't about letting other people dictate her path but about gaining insight into how others perceived her strengths and qualities.

What she discovered wasn't something new or shocking but confirmation of what she already felt yet hadn't fully embraced. That's the power of asking for external perspectives. Others' opinions do not define your purpose, but they shed light on areas you might overlook or doubt.

Reflection
- **Pick your people wisely**: Choose three to five people whose opinions you respect. These people should know your journey, growth, and character, perhaps mentors, friends, family members, or leaders who've supported you through challenges. But be careful because people project. Without realizing it, some people will answer through the lens of their experiences or fears. This doesn't mean their input isn't valuable, but you must filter it. That's why it's important to focus on *how they see you* and not *what they think you*

should do. We're all human, and even the best-intentioned people can project their doubts, dreams, and expectations onto others.
- **Ask insightful questions:** Don't ask them what you should do. Instead, ask questions like:
  - *What do you think I'm naturally good at?*
  - *What qualities do you see in me that stand out?*
  - *How would you describe me to someone who doesn't know me?*
- **Reflect, don't react**: When you receive their feedback, don't rush to agree or disagree. Just take it in. Later, reflect on how their responses align with what you already know about yourself. Remember, this isn't about seeking validation but gaining perspective.
- **Look for consistency:** Pay attention to recurring themes. If multiple people point out the same strength or quality, that's worth noting. Their feedback may help you uncover a part of your purpose that you hadn't fully recognized.

WHY THIS MATTERS

Clarity often comes when you least expect it and hearing how others view you can be a powerful tool in that process. My sister's experience taught me that we're often too close to ourselves to see clearly. When you gather trusted feedback, you're not giving others control but gathering pieces of a puzzle that only you can put together. If you're feeling stuck, this exercise may help you connect the dots.

Reflection

- **Your changing why:** Identify your big "why," the one that drives you long-term. Now, list three smaller "whys" that you can tackle on tough days. These can be as simple as proving something to yourself, achieving a short-term goal, or setting an example for someone who looks up to you.

CHAPTER THREE: ALIGNING ACTIONS WITH PURPOSE

Finding your purpose is only the beginning. Once you know what drives you, you must begin to show up. Purpose doesn't mean anything if it just stays in your head. That's where a lot of people get it wrong. They think that once they find their purpose, the hard part is over. But purpose without action is just a dream. Purpose isn't real until you're living it, breathing it, and making it a part of who you are.

For me, purpose became real once I started showing up and doing the work, even on the days I didn't feel like it. I wasn't just talking about "No Excuse" because it sounded good. I was living it. Back in college, I'd post a Snapchat story every morning. This was something I did to keep myself accountable, but over time, people started to depend on it. If I missed a day, my phone would light up with messages.

Where's the post?

Are you okay?

I had become part of their routine, too, and they were looking to me for motivation, and that fueled me further.

Those Snapchat posts weren't anything fancy, just me talking to the camera, showing people I was up early, putting in the work, and challenging them to do the same. I wasn't putting on a show. Instead, I was sharing genuine thoughts. Over time, people relied on my posts to kick-start their day. That taught me a valuable lesson: When you live out your purpose consistently, you're lifting up everyone who's watching, those who look to you for that push to keep going. When you live out your purpose, your purpose becomes a part of you. It shows up in how you talk, how you walk, and how you handle yourself. And trust me, people notice.

MAKING PURPOSE A PART OF YOUR DAILY ROUTINE

To live out your purpose, you must make your purpose a part of your daily routine. Your routine doesn't have to be complicated. Perhaps it's a small but steady action, one that births the greatest impact. Here's how you can start aligning your daily actions with your purpose:

1. **Set daily intentions**. Before you start your day, remind yourself of your "why." Think about how you'll live it out that day. It could be something as simple as committing yourself to one action that reflects your purpose.
2. **Reflect on your actions**. At the end of the day, ask yourself if you lived in alignment with your purpose. Did your actions reflect your beliefs? If not, what can you do tomorrow?
3. **Create non-negotiables**. Find actions you'll commit to daily, no matter what. These are your non-negotiables. My non-negotiable

was working out. So, I made sure I put in the work. Figure out your non-negotiables and stick to them.
4. **Track your progress**. Purpose isn't something you find and forget. So, keep a journal, track your actions, and gauge your growth over time. It's not about perfection but progress.

THE CHALLENGES OF STAYING ALIGNED

Let's get real. Staying aligned with your purpose won't be a straight line. There will be times when you doubt yourself, the path forward looks foggy, and it feels like you're moving backward. I know what that's like. After I moved to Orlando, I thought I had everything figured out. I was ready to make it big, but things didn't go the way I planned. No longer in Jersey with my client base, I had to start over, rebuild my clientele, and prove myself all over again.

There were days I wondered if I had made the right move or if I should've stayed where I was established. But every time I thought about giving up, I remembered why I started. I wasn't in this for a quick win. I was in Orlando to make a real impact and show people that there's no excuse for giving up. And that's what kept me going.

Purpose isn't about avoiding challenges but pushing through them because you know that what's on the other side is worth it. Every setback I faced and every time I had to adjust my plans, I was forced to grow. That's when I realized purpose doesn't always look the way you expect, and that's okay. What matters is that you stay true to it, even when the path twists and turns.

EMBRACING ADAPTABILITY IN PURPOSE

Sometimes, you think you've got it all figured out, and life throws you a curveball. That's not a sign to give up. It's a reminder to stay adaptable. When I moved to Orlando, everything moved quickly. My life felt renewed with opportunities and connections. I felt like I had stepped into the life I had been working toward. But just because life was going well didn't mean the past disappeared. I was still learning to be responsible. At that time, I was earning more money than ever, but I didn't know how to manage it. I was living fast and enjoying my wins, but the real world kept spinning. Lawyer bills started piling up, as I still had past fees to pay. Before I knew it, my money was flying out the window just as fast as it was coming in. Then came the collection calls, one after the other. I felt a nudge from God, as if He were saying "Don't get too comfortable yet."

That was a major wake-up call. I had to readjust my game plan, stop living in the moment, and start handling my business to walk responsibly in my purpose. Each time I've had to adapt, I gained a new perspective. I've learned that it's not about sticking to a rigid plan but staying committed to the core of what drives you.

Purpose is like a compass. It points you in the right direction, but you still have to navigate around the obstacles. You must be willing to take detours, adjust your sails, and keep moving forward, no matter what. Whether I'm training in a backyard or coaching top clients, my purpose hasn't changed. I'm here to inspire, push boundaries, and live a life without excuses. And as long as I stay true to that, I know I'm on the right path.

CHAPTER FOUR: OVERCOMING SETBACKS AND STAYING MOTIVATED

When you're on a mission, you must accept that setbacks are a part of the journey. The path isn't smooth, and it's not supposed to be. You'll hit walls and face days when nothing goes right, and it'll feel like the world is against you. Remember that purpose doesn't make life easier; it makes life worth it.

Back at my No Excuse Factory in my backyard, I'd often look around at the muddy ground and rusty weights, and I'd question if pursuing this goal was worth it. But purpose doesn't care about comfort. My backyard wasn't just a place to train. It was a proving ground. Every day I went out there, I was proving to myself that I could do it.

And that's what purpose demands.

It asks you to prove it, every single day.

Setbacks will test your resolve and force you to dig deeper than you thought possible. But here's the thing: Setbacks aren't just obstacles, they're opportunities. Every time you face a setback, you have a chance to learn, adapt, and come back stronger and wiser. Purpose doesn't promise an easy road. It promises a meaningful one. And if you're willing to embrace the grind and face setbacks head-on, you'll find that each challenge is shaping you into the person you need to be.

STRATEGIES FOR STAYING MOTIVATED THROUGH SETBACKS

Motivation isn't about hype or feeling good but finding ways to keep moving forward. Here's what works for me when the going gets tough:

1. **Find the lesson in the struggle**. Every setback offers a lesson. When plans fall apart, ask yourself, "What am I supposed to learn from this?" The sooner you find the lesson, the quicker you can turn that setback into a steppingstone. A mindset shift will keep you from getting stuck in a negative loop and helps you move forward with a clearer perspective.
2. **Break it down and get tactical**. If the big picture feels overwhelming, break it down. Focus on the next step, then the one after that. Don't worry about tomorrow or next week. Focus on winning the day, and those small wins will add up over time.
3. **Leverage the power of visual reminders**. Sometimes, you need a visual reminder to keep you locked in. Find something that represents your "why," whether a photo, quote, or a tangible object. Keep it where you can see it, and when life gets rough, let that reminder re-center you.
4. **Redefine failure and keep moving forward**. People see setbacks as failure, but real failure only happens when you quit. If you're still in the game, you're still learning, adapting, and building resilience.

Redefining failure as part of the process helps you push through when life doesn't go your way.

5. **Use pain as fuel**. Pain is a powerful motivator. Don't shy away from it. Lean into it! Let the tough moments remind you why you're in this fight. Pain can break you down or build you up; you must decide. When you let pain fuel your drive, you'll become an unstoppable force.

THE BRUTAL HONESTY OF PURPOSE

Here's the truth: Purpose isn't glamorous. Purpose doesn't make life easier. In fact, it makes life harder because you've got something to lose. Living with purpose means you're not coasting. You're pushing and grinding, and sometimes, you're suffering. But that's what makes it real.

There were times I was dead broke, wondering if I was wasting my time, and times when people doubted me and said I wouldn't make it. Every setback felt like confirmation of their doubts. But purpose isn't about how you feel on your worst days. It's about what you do on those challenging days. It's about getting up and fighting when you're tired or in doubt. Because deep down, you know that giving up isn't an option.

Purpose asks for everything you've got and then some. It's not a game or a hobby but a commitment. You're going to lose sleep and some friends, and you're going to question if pursuing your purpose is worth the loss. But that's when you dig deep and remember that you didn't come this far to give up.

So, if you're going to live with purpose, be ready for frequent reality checks. Be ready to face setbacks and feel pain and keep pushing because that's what separates those who talk from those who act. Become the person you were meant to be, one struggle at a time.

WHY IT'S WORTH IT TO LIVE IN YOUR PURPOSE

Yeah, I know, after reading all of that, you might be wondering if pursuing your purpose is worth it. Well, let me tell you straight up. Pursuing your purpose is worth every bit of struggle. Living in your purpose doesn't mean life gets easier. It means life becomes meaningful.

There's a difference.

Without purpose, you can go through life aimlessly, surviving day to day, hoping for something to change. But when you have purpose, you're not just living, you're building. Every setback becomes a lesson, every loss becomes a steppingstone, and every long night and early morning become fuel for something greater. You stop existing and start living.

I grew up in East Orange at a time when people were robbed or shot every week. The city was nicknamed "Baby Newark," demonstrating a frightening similarity to Newark, a city that was considered one of the top ten most dangerous cities in the nation. I wondered if this was all my life was meant to be. But something inside me refused to settle. Something kept telling me there has to be more. That fire to pursue more was purpose whispering in my ear, pushing me forward.

Fast forward. I'm training NBA athletes and celebrities. I'm sitting courtside at NBA games, enjoying luxuries I didn't know were possible. But let me be clear: Money and access do not define success. The real win is who I've become. It's the peace I have, knowing I'm walking in my purpose. I no longer feel the weight of regret on my chest because I took control of my life, built something out of nothing, and didn't allow my past to dictate my future.

Imagine how young Randy, walking around East Orange, would feel seeing this. He'd smile from ear to ear, proud as ever, knowing he made it out. I pray my father is proudly looking down from Heaven. I hope he's up there saying, "That's my boy. He didn't just survive. He thrived." Life is certainly sweeter because I'm no longer chasing validation from strangers. Instead, I validate myself through my impact in others' lives. That's what purpose does. It gives you something to fight for when circumstances tell you to give up.

When you live in your purpose, you also attract the right people. You start surrounding yourself with others who are on their own journey, understand the grind, and see your hustle and respect it. Purpose connects you with people who will pour into you, challenge you, and want to see you win. Purpose builds a tribe, community, and a support system. And that's priceless.

Here's another reason why pursuing your purpose is worth the struggle: Your legacy. Living with purpose means that long after you're gone, what you built and stood for will remain. It means your name will be mentioned in rooms you'll never step into. It means the lives you touch today will ripple far beyond what you can see, so remember that you're not just living for today; you're building for tomorrow and years to come.

Live in your purpose not because it's easy, but because it's necessary. Not because it guarantees success, but because it guarantees growth. Not because it's glamorous, but because it's real. And trust me, real always wins.

CHAPTER FIVE: STAYING TRUE TO YOUR PURPOSE DESPITE EXTERNAL PRESSURES

When you're committed to a path, not everyone is going to get it. You'll face doubt, criticism, and people who will try to talk you out of it. They'll claim they're looking out for you, but they're usually speaking from a place of fear. These pressures can come from anyone—friends, family, mentors, or people you once looked up to. And when those doubts come from people you respect, it hits different. You start questioning if they're right or if you're the one who's missing something.

I remember when I announced that I was moving to Florida. So many people I admired, people I thought would support me, tried to put fear in my heart. They said things like, "Are you sure you're ready for this? The fitness world is tough down there." Or they'd disguise their thoughts as concern: "I just want to make sure you're prepared for the real world." But the thing is, life has already prepared me for this. They didn't know the battles I'd already fought and the challenges I'd already faced. I didn't need their doubts clouding my mind. So, I'd have to stop them mid-conversation. They'd assure me they were trying to help, not realizing I had already been through more than they could imagine.

That's the thing about purpose. You have to be so confident in it that you can stand firm, even when those you respect begin to question you. When you're living out your purpose, you'll eventually have to defend it. You must be ready to say "no" when others try to project their fears onto you. It takes strength to stay grounded in your vision and to let their doubts bounce off you without letting it shake your foundation.

HOW TO STAY TRUE TO YOUR PURPOSE IN THE FACE OF DOUBT

1. **Know your why inside and out**. The deeper you understand your "why," the easier it is to stand firm. When external pressures start to weigh you down, your purpose becomes your anchor. Remind yourself what drives you. Replay that motivation over and over. When you have a firm grip on your "why," it won't matter who questions you. Your purpose is yours, and nobody can take that from you.
2. **Build a strong inner circle**. You need people who get it, who understand what you're about, and won't let you lose sight. This isn't about having a bunch of yes-men around. It's about surrounding yourself with people who know your vision and will challenge you to stay true to it. Those people become your shield when outside pressures creep in. We'll dive deeper into this topic in

a later chapter but know that your circle must be rock solid. Not everyone deserves a spot. Choose wisely.

3. **Stay focused on the big picture**. When you're hit with doubt and criticism, zoom out. Look at where you're headed, not where you are. Opinions are temporary, but purpose is lasting. When people try to throw you off track, remind yourself of the long game. Their doubts don't change your destination. Keep your eyes on the bigger picture, and let the small stuff roll off your back.

4. **Be ready to walk alone**. Sometimes, you'll have to walk alone. Staying true to your purpose means accepting that not everyone's going to be on board. Don't let the fear of walking alone make you compromise. Your path is yours to walk, and that means walking solo sometimes. Strength lies in being comfortable to stand alone.

PERSONAL EXAMPLE: STANDING FIRM IN THE FACE OF DOUBT

My move to Orlando was a turning point. People thought I was throwing away my success. They questioned why I'd give up what I built in Jersey, but I knew I needed to take the leap. I couldn't stay comfortable, even if that meant I needed to start from scratch. I had conversations where I had to defend my decision and outright say, "I don't want to hear your doubts." I'd have to cut through their negativity because I knew they were projecting their fears, and I wasn't about to let that dictate my path.

This wasn't easy, especially when the doubts came from people I looked up to, but I knew that I'd rather walk my path alone than stay somewhere just to make other people comfortable. I wasn't going to let anyone's fears become my reality. I had already been through enough to know that I could handle whatever came my way. So, I took a risk, knowing that the only opinion that truly mattered was my own.

ANOTHER HONEST TRUTH OF PURPOSE

Here's the truth: Purpose is lonely. It's raw, gritty, and not always glamorous. People will try to talk you out of it, not because they don't care, but because they don't understand. They'll disguise fear as advice, and if you're not careful, you'll believe it. Purpose demands that you stand firm, block out the noise, and stay focused.

You must be willing to let people walk away if they can't handle the path you're on. Purpose isn't about keeping everyone happy. It's about staying true to yourself, even when you have to go against the grain. You'll have to ignore the noise, walk away from the doubters, and hold on to your purpose like it's the only thing that matters. Because, at the end of the day, it is. People think purpose is all about passion and inspiration, but they forget about the pain. They forget that living with purpose means sacrificing comfort and relationships. But if you're truly committed, you'll find a way to push through.

Here's more truth: Purpose isn't about pleasing others or fitting in. It's about standing strong, even when you must stand alone. It's about facing doubts, staring down fear, and saying, "I'm here to stay." Purpose is raw, real, and relentless, but it's worth every ounce of struggle, every lonely step, and every doubt you have to overcome.

CHAPTER SIX: EMBRACING DISCOMFORT AND HARD WORK

PART I: THE GRIND IS NON-NEGOTIABLE

People want success, but most don't want to do what it takes to achieve it. They ask God for results and a breakthrough, but they forget a crucial element: Faith without works is dead (James 2:26). You can have all the faith in the world, but if you're not willing to put in the work, nothing will happen. God won't hand you success on a silver platter. You have to get up, put in the effort, and show that you're serious.

That's where the grind comes in. And here's the truth: The grind is non-negotiable.

The grind doesn't care about your feelings or whether you're motivated. The grind is about showing up and pushing through discomfort. This isn't just about physical effort. It's mental, emotional, and spiritual. If you're chasing a big goal, you'll be tested, and in that discomfort is where growth takes place.

But let's talk about the embarrassment factor.

I don't think enough people talk about this.

There's a certain feeling of shame that comes with starting over and not having everything together. People may see where I'm at now, but many don't know of my humble beginnings. Of course, there were times I felt embarrassed by the setup and by the fact that I wasn't where I wanted to be.

What I've learned is that embarrassment is a part of the journey and the grind. Embarrassment forces you to confront your insecurities and push past the fear of what others might think.

And guess what?

Starting over is embarrassing, too. It's tough to admit when something isn't working, to let go of what's familiar, and to begin again. But that's part of the process. Too many people are afraid of looking foolish, so they never try. But if you're worried about how you look, you won't grow. Get comfortable being uncomfortable, even when it feels like everyone's watching.

Reflection
- **Identify your grind**: What's hard in your life that you've been avoiding? Whether it's a personal goal, career move, or relationship issue, write it down. Ask yourself why you've been avoiding it and how you can lean into that discomfort.
- **Challenge your embarrassment**: Think about a time when you felt embarrassed or worried about what others thought of you. How did

those feelings affect your decision(s)? What would you do differently if you didn't care about others' opinions? Write a plan for how you can push past that fear in a future situation.

LEANING INTO DISCOMFORT IS THE ONLY WAY FORWARD

Discomfort isn't something to avoid but a signal that you're on the right path. If you're not uncomfortable, you're not growing. This lesson hit me hard when I wasn't seeing the results I expected early on. I was grinding every day, putting in hours with clients, but things weren't clicking—money wasn't flowing like I thought it would, clients weren't rolling in, and financial stress was worsening because bills don't stop while the grind unfolds. That's when I had to remind myself that the grind doesn't care about immediate results. It cares about consistency and trusting the process.

I always tell my clients that they won't lose ten pounds in one workout. The human body doesn't work that way. Weight loss, muscle gains, and improved fitness come from a collection of consistent actions. Physical improvement is the combination of workouts, a nutrition plan, and daily intentionality. You won't see immediate results from one day of effort but as a compound effect of everything you do over time. One workout, one meal, one decision to push through—those add up. The results won't come overnight, but they will come. The key is to trust the process and stay consistent, even when progress seems slow.

A quote that hit home for me came from Steve Harvey, who said, "If you're going through hell, keep going." That's the essence of embracing discomfort, to keep moving no matter how you feel. You will face moments when quitting seems like the best option, but you must remember that those moments are tests to reveal how badly you want to achieve success.

Reflection
- **Track your small wins**. Think about a big goal you've been working on toward achieving. Break the goal down into smaller, daily wins. How can you stack those small wins to create momentum? Write down three small actions you can take every day for the next week that will move you closer to your goal.
- **Commit to consistency**. What area of your life have you been inconsistent? Whether it's fitness, work, or relationships, write down why you haven't been consistent and what's been holding you back. Now, create a plan for how you'll show up daily.

WINNING THE BATTLE IN YOUR HEAD

The most important battle you'll ever fight is the one in your head. People talk about the grind like it's only physical, but the mental grind is where most people lose. The mind will play tricks on you. It'll tell you that you're not good enough, that you're wasting your time, and that the results won't come. And if you're not careful, you'll believe those thoughts. In fact, there's science behind this. Studies show that 95% of our thoughts are repetitive, with 80% of them being negative. This aligns with research on Repetitive Negative Thinking (RNT), which includes patterns such as rumination and worry and plays a key role in anxiety, depression, and other mental health challenges. So, the majority of what's running through your head daily is self-doubt, fear, and limiting beliefs.

How do you win that battle?

By training your mind the same way you train your body—with discipline, repetition, and focus. You must challenge your negative thoughts and replace them with positive actions.

This is where mental endurance comes in. Teach your mind to keep going. The more you push through, the stronger your mental resilience becomes. And believe me, the battle in your head is far tougher than anything you'll face physically. It's easy to work when you're motivated, but what about when your mind tells you to quit? That's where discipline comes into play.

Mike Tyson once said, "Discipline is doing what you hate to do, but nonetheless doing it like you love it." It's not about feeling like doing the work; it's about showing up regardless of how you feel. That's the only way to push past mental roadblocks. Every time you overcome the voice in your head that tells you to stop, you become stronger. And the stronger you become, the more power you'll have to take on bigger challenges without getting shaken.

Reflection
- **Tame your negative thoughts**: Write down the negative, repetitive thoughts you have about yourself. For each negative thought, write a counter-thought, something positive that challenges your negative belief. Commit to replacing every negative thought with a positive thought for the next 30 days.

- **Build mental endurance**. Just like you train your body, you need to train your mind. Write down one mental challenge you frequently experience. It could be waking up early, committing to a workout, or completing a difficult task at work. Track your progress and gauge how your mental strength grows over time.

LIFE WILL TEST YOU TO SEE HOW BADLY YOU WANT IT

Here's something I've always said: Life will always test you to see how badly you actually want it. You can't say you want something without acknowledging that you'll be tested for it. That's just how life works. The grind is designed to make you prove how much you're willing to endure to get what you say you want.

Think about it. Life will always throw something at you to see if you're truly committed. This curveball might be a setback, failure, or personal challenge. Whatever it is, it will test your resolve. Those tests aren't there to break you but to see if you'll keep going when life gets tough. And believe me, life will get tough.

You can't avoid the test, but you can prepare for it. That's why discipline is critical. When I say, "You don't rise to the occasion; you fall back on the habits you've built," I mean that when challenges arise, you won't suddenly perform at your best just because the situation demands it. Instead, you'll perform based on routine, discipline, and habits.

For example, if you've been consistent in your training, your body will know what to do when it's time to compete because it's been there before. But if you've been slacking, you can't expect to suddenly perform at a high level just because the stakes are higher. The same goes for life. When stress, pressure, or unexpected situations arise, you'll naturally default to the patterns and mindset you've been reinforcing all along.

Reflection
- **Prepare for the test**: Think about a recent setback or challenge. How did you handle it? Write down three ways to better prepare yourself mentally and emotionally for future challenges.

PART II: SACRIFICES AND TRADE-OFFS

If you're serious about success, you need to be serious about sacrifice. No matter how much talent you have, how much support you receive, or how much faith you carry, there's always a cost to greatness, and if you're not willing to pay that price, then you're not really committed.

People love the idea of success. They love the spotlight, recognition, and financial freedom. But what they don't talk about are the sacrifices behind the scenes. Sacrifice doesn't just mean giving up time or money; it means giving up comfort. Success forces you to choose between what you want now and what you want most. It's a constant trade-off, and the deeper you go into the grind, the more you realize there's no avoiding sacrifice.

Moving from New Jersey to Orlando was one of the biggest trade-offs I ever made. But here's the thing: Success isn't about staying comfortable. It's about pushing yourself into new territory where you're not certain what will happen next. I knew that staying in New Jersey meant playing it safe, but I didn't want safe. I wanted more. And to get more, I had to sacrifice. That was my trade-off. If you're not willing to give up good for great, you'll remain stagnant.

AN INTERVIEW SERIES WITH CLARISE SIMMONS

Were there moments when you doubted yourself and considered staying in New Jersey?

Absolutely. I'd be lying if I said I didn't question myself countless times before making the move. There were nights when I sat in my room, staring at the ceiling, wondering if I was making the biggest mistake of my life. Imagine working hard for years, finally having some stability, and then thinking about throwing that away to start over. At the same time, I had the opportunity to train a pro-level athlete, something many people dream of. But here's the thing. I didn't want to live with the regret of wondering "what if?" That thought haunted me more than the fear of failure. Staying would've been the easier choice, but easy doesn't change your life. Easy doesn't elevate you. I had to take a leap, not because I wasn't scared, but because I was more afraid of wondering what could've been.

How did you progress when doubt crept in?

Doubt didn't visit once. It moved in. There were moments when the weight of uncertainty felt suffocating. But I reminded myself of one thing: Progress isn't about waiting until you feel ready. It's about moving forward when everything inside you is screaming to stop. I kept telling myself, "If you quit now, what was all that grind for?" And you know what? I leaned on my circle during those moments. I didn't need people to hype me up. I needed people to remind me who I was when I forgot. That's why having the right people around you is crucial. They won't let you sink into your doubts. They pull you out and push you forward.

How did you handle losses during this transition?

Man, losses hit hard. I lost clients and financial stability, and I felt like I was losing a part of myself. It's tough when you finally get used to winning, and suddenly, it feels like life is handing you L after L. But I realized that losses aren't permanent unless you let them. Every setback and loss was a lesson disguised as pain. When I lost clients, I didn't sit around feeling sorry for myself. I got to work to find new ones. When I lost my financial cushion, I used that hunger to push harder. The emotional toll? Yeah, that was real. There were days when I felt drained, wondering if it was all worth it. But every loss forced me to grow in ways I never would have if I stayed comfortable. I had to start viewing losses as stepping stones. You don't grow without pain, and you don't succeed without setbacks.

How did you have enough faith to move forward despite everything?

Trusting God and knowing if this fails, I made it out of situations and circumstances that were way worse. Faith came from looking back on all the battles I already won. There were so many moments I thought,

"This is it. I'm done." But somehow, I always made it through. That's what faith is—knowing that if you survived the last storm, you'll survive the next one, too. Let me keep it real, though. My faith wasn't always strong. There were days when my faith was barely holding on, but I showed up anyway. That's key. Faith isn't about having all the answers but about moving forward, even when you can't see the whole path. It's about trusting that your effort, grind, and heart are enough to get you where you're meant to be.

I prayed a lot during times of uncertainty and amid transitions, asking God for strength, guidance, and clarity to keep going. And every time I wanted to quit, something would happen—a random word of encouragement from someone, a small win, or a quiet moment when I felt peace that reminded me to keep going. Faith isn't always loud. Sometimes, it's a quiet nudge that you're going to make it.

FINAL THOUGHTS: PAYING THE PRICE FOR GREATNESS

Sacrifices and trade-offs aren't optional if you want to achieve greatness. They're part of the deal, but what you gain in return is worth the sacrifice. The cost of success is high, but the regret of staying the same is higher. I'm not telling you this to scare you. I'm telling you this because it's real. If you're willing to pay the price and keep pushing when the world feels like it's against you, then what's waiting on the other side will be worth every tear, loss, and moment of doubt. The question is, are you ready to pay the price?

THE REAL COST OF SACRIFICE

The truth about sacrifice is that it's not a one-time deal. Sacrifice is ongoing. It's about sacrificing now in the hope that what you gain later will be worth it. It means late nights, early mornings, missing out on time with friends and family, and sometimes putting your personal life on hold to focus on the goal. You have to sacrifice old habits, routines, and versions of yourself. You can't reach new heights while holding on to the same behaviors. You have to let go of the familiar to make room for what's next. And believe me, that's not easy. The familiar is comfortable, but comfort is the enemy of progress.

The people closest to me understood this. They saw my determination and knew I wasn't making sacrifices for nothing. But not everyone outside of my inner circle understood. There were plenty of people who questioned why I was putting my energy into something that didn't have clear returns. What they didn't see was the bigger picture, the future I was working toward.

WHAT DOES IT MEAN TO GIVE UP PEOPLE?

Giving up people doesn't mean cutting ties out of spite or anger. It means recognizing when certain relationships no longer serve your growth. Sometimes, people who were a part of your journey are not meant to go with you to the next level. It's not about being better than anyone but prioritizing your peace, growth, and goals. Letting go can be hard, especially when you share history with someone. But holding onto relationships that drain you or hold you back will only slow down your progress.

HOW DO YOU KNOW WHO TO GIVE UP?

You'll know it's time to let go of someone when their presence starts to feel like a weight. Pay attention to how you feel after spending time with them. Are you motivated and inspired, or do you feel drained and discouraged? Do they celebrate your wins or get quiet when you succeed? Are they constantly bringing negativity into your life or making you second-guess yourself? If the people around you aren't contributing to your growth, it's time to reevaluate their role in your life.

WHAT DOES AN UNSUPPORTIVE PERSON LOOK LIKE?

An unsupportive person doesn't have to be openly negative. Sometimes, negativity is subtle. They might dismiss your goals, make sarcastic comments about your ambitions, or constantly remind you of your past mistakes. They may only hit you up when they need something but disappear when you're the one in need. Toxic people thrive on keeping you where you are because your growth makes them uncomfortable. They might guilt trip you for focusing on your goals or accuse you of "changing" as if change is a bad thing. A true friend supports your growth, even if that means seeing less of you because your goals occupy your time, and they cheer you on from the sidelines. If someone can't respect your hustle, they shouldn't be a part of your future.

KNOWING WHEN TO LET GO

Letting go doesn't have to be dramatic. Letting go can be as simple as creating distance. You don't have to announce that you're cutting someone off. Just start focusing on your goals, and you'll notice that the right people will stay, and the wrong ones will drift away. Protecting your energy is crucial, and that means making tough choices about who can stay in your life. Remember, you can't grow if you're surrounded by people who don't want to see you win. Sacrificing relationships that no longer align with your purpose is part of the journey. It's not easy but necessary. At the end of the day, your future is more important than holding onto people who are stuck in the past.

THE TRADE-OFFS: WHAT ARE YOU WILLING TO GIVE UP?

Every success story is full of trade-offs. The question you have to ask yourself is: what are you willing to give up to get where you want to go? Are you willing to sacrifice comfort for growth? Are you willing to let go of the familiar to reach for something bigger? These trade-offs are where most people fall short. They want success, but they're not willing to trade anything for it. They want the rewards without the sacrifice.

When I started building my business, I had to sacrifice my personal life. I didn't make this decision lightly, but I knew that if I wanted to be the best, I had to go all in. That meant less time socializing and more time grinding. I didn't just cut out distractions; I cut out excuses. And that's what a lot of people don't understand. Every excuse you hold onto is a trade-off, something that takes the place of your progress.

One thing I had to take a break from was partying. And while that sacrifice may sound simple, you'd understand how big this was for me if you knew me during my younger days. I was a partier, an entertainer. I loved to party, dance, and be the light in the room. At my core, I enjoy bringing people together and creating a good time. That's just who I am. If you're from Essex County, you know what I'm talking about. Everyone was a dancer. We grew up on Jersey Club music—a fast-paced, high-energy genre that's all about rhythm and movement. It's more than just music; it's a culture. I used to be a part of a dance team called BandzUp. We'd battle, perform, and light up the floor. Dancing and partying weren't just hobbies. They were a part of my identity, so giving that up was tough. It's what I knew, what I grew up on. But I also knew those parties would always be there. The clubs, music, and fun—those weren't going anywhere. Locking in on my goals had to be the priority. I'd rather sacrifice those nights and enjoy them later than indulge now and regret it later. That's the mindset needed to achieve success—temporary sacrifices for permanent growth. Every day is a chance to trade your current comfort for future success.

Reflection
- **Identify your trade-offs**: What are you willing to give up to achieve your goals? Whether it's time, money, or comfort, write down what you need to sacrifice to get where you want to be.

- **Evaluate your sacrifices**: Reflect on a recent trade-off you made. Was the sacrifice worth it? How did this sacrifice impact your progress, and would you make this decision again? Reflecting on this will help you assess whether your sacrifices align with your long-term goals.
- **Commit to the long game**: Sacrifice isn't just about short-term discomfort but about remaining consistent for the long haul. Write down three long-term sacrifices you're committed to making to inch closer to your vision.

PART III: LOVING THE PROCESS

One of the hardest facts to accept is that success does not come from simply reaching the goal but from embracing the process. Most people fixate on outcomes, like money and popularity, but they're not in love with the journey. The daily work, small wins, setbacks, and failures are all a part of the process. If you're only focused on the end result, you'll feel discouraged when success doesn't happen as fast as you want. But if you fall in love with the process, you can keep going, even when progress is slow.

This lesson came early for me in my career. When I was training in my backyard, I had to fall in love with what I was doing every day. It wasn't about the paycheck or recognition. It was about knowing that I was getting stronger, better, and closer to where I wanted to be. My clients didn't care about my backyard setup because they saw the results, and that fueled me.

But even with focus and determination, I hit a point of depression. I was so fixated on hitting big wins that I forgot about small daily victories. When those big wins didn't come as fast as I thought they should, I started being hard on myself. I felt like I was doing all this work for nothing. I've always been hard on myself, which isn't always a bad thing. High expectations help me work harder. In sports, high expectations helped me dominate my competition. However, the imbalance can backfire, and it definitely did when the journey of being an entrepreneur wasn't working in my favor. I would curse myself out in my head, calling myself every name in the book. I'd get so frustrated that I'd have to hit the gym just to keep from smashing my laptop. (Let's not forget, I had serious anger issues as a kid, and sometimes those feelings crept back in.) I'd start spiraling with thoughts like, "What am I doing this for and why isn't this working?" I was so consumed with the bigger picture that I completely overlooked my progress. The truth was, I was changing lives. I had current and past clients reaching out, telling me how much I impacted their lives.

How could I overlook that?

Probably because I was too focused on the bigger outcome instead of appreciating daily wins. After all, those daily wins got me started on this journey in the first place. But I lost sight of that when I became obsessed with how quickly I wanted to reach my larger goals.

BRUTAL HONESTY: LEARN TO ADJUST OR ACCEPT DEFEAT

Here's the brutal truth: I have days when I feel overwhelmed, like I'm being pulled in a million directions, and no matter how much I accomplish, it doesn't feel like enough. I've had moments where I've felt unproductive and needed to reset my mind. That's reality. No matter how disciplined or committed you are, there will be days when you need to recalibrate. But here's the key: Resetting doesn't mean quitting. Resetting means adjusting. Sometimes, all it takes is a change of environment to get your head back in the game. When I'm training clients and the fitness grind starts to feel routine, I switch it up. We'll hit the track instead of the gym or try a new workout to keep things fresh. If you're in a different profession, consider taking your client to lunch instead of having a standard office meeting, just to shake things up. Changing the vibe and environment can re-energize you and the people you're working with.

Successful people know how to adjust. That's something I learned from one of the greatest fighters of all time, Floyd Mayweather. In boxing, the best fighters know how to adjust mid-fight. They read their opponent, recognize what's working and what isn't, and adapt. If you feel like you're in the middle of warfare, make adjustments in the middle of the battle. Change your strategy and environment and find what works.

Success isn't just about grinding it out blindly but knowing when and how to adjust. That's the difference between burning out and winning. So, if you're feeling stuck, overwhelmed, or unproductive, take a step back. Determine which adjustments need to be made to keep moving forward.

Reflection

- **Find joy in the process**: Write down the steps in your journey that you've been avoiding because they don't seem enjoyable. How can you find joy in the daily grind? What mindset shift do you need to make to start loving the process, not just the outcome?
- **Make adjustments**: Think about a current situation where you feel stuck or unproductive. How can you adjust your environment or routine to re-energize? Write down a few changes you can make this week to switch things up and keep your momentum going.

PART IV: THE BRUTAL TRUTH OF OVERWHELM AND ADJUSTING IN THE PROCESS

The truth people don't often discuss is that overwhelm is inevitable. No matter how disciplined, motivated, or driven, there will be days when life feels heavy. After all, we aren't robots. Pressure piles up, and even the most successful people reach a point when they wonder if they're doing enough or if their effort is worth it. People look at those who seem to have it all and assume their path was smooth, but the grind will bring anyone to the edge at some point. What separates those who thrive from those who fall off is knowing how to manage overwhelm.

There are moments in my life when everything feels like it's coming at me from all angles—clients needing attention, personal commitments, financial pressure, health goals, and the constant demands of life. Feeling overwhelmed doesn't make someone weak.

Acknowledgement is the first step toward finding balance and regaining control. Those who succeed learn to pivot, adjust, and push forward, even when their mind screams for a break.

One critical lesson to understand is that feeling unproductive doesn't equal failure. There are days when it seems like nothing is moving forward and the to-do list looks the same at the end of the day as it did in the morning. The feeling of spinning in place is frustrating but understand that growth happens amid the pauses and reflections. This is where intentionality comes into play. A person can grind all day, but if their direction isn't clear, their effort will go to waste. Resetting the mind will be the difference between spinning in circles and moving forward with purpose.

TAKING TIME TO RESET

In today's hustle culture, guilt is often tied to taking time off. The pressure to constantly be in motion makes it hard to justify a period dedicated to recharging. But there's wisdom in recognizing when the body and mind need a break. Even the most disciplined athletes, entrepreneurs, and leaders know that you can't pour from an empty cup. Trying to grind at 50% doesn't serve anyone, especially not the person aiming for excellence.

No one can be at their best all the time.

There's value in stepping back, unplugging, and resetting. Resetting doesn't mean permanently stopping. It means recharging for the next phase. For anyone chasing success, rest and reset are part of the grind.

During your reset, consider a change of scenery to spark new energy and ideas. Go on a hike, hit the gym, or remain still, all of which shift and calm the mind. It's not about abandoning the grind but acknowledging your feelings and recharging appropriately. This is how longevity is cultivated and sustained.

ADJUSTING IN THE PROCESS: THE KEY TO LONGEVITY

There's a reason why some people thrive in any situation while others fall apart at the first sign of resistance. It's not because the grind is easier for them but because they know how to adjust. Flexibility is a weapon in the fight for success.

A great example of this comes from the world of business. Look at Jeff Bezos, founder of Amazon. When he first started, Amazon was just an online bookstore. But Bezos didn't remain stuck in that original vision. He paid attention to market trends, customer demands, and new opportunities. As the world changed, he adjusted Amazon's focus, expanding into electronics, cloud computing, and entertainment. His ability to pivot and adapt turned Amazon from a small online bookstore into one of the most profitable companies in the world. And that's key—recognizing when something isn't working and having the courage to shift gears. It's not about abandoning your goals but finding new paths to reach them. Adjusting is a sign of resilience. It's about staying committed to your purpose while remaining flexible in your approach. Adaptability separates those who succeed from those who fall behind.

Whether you're running a business, at the office, training clients, or navigating personal challenges, the ability to adjust keeps the process moving. There will be moments when the original plan no longer makes sense and when the strategy that seemed flawless suddenly stops working. That's when adjustments have to be made. The plan might need to shift, and tactics may need tweaking, but the vision remains the same.

Stubbornly sticking to one way of doing things can be risky. Those who refuse to adapt when life throws curveballs often stay stuck. Progress requires flexibility to adjust strategies while staying committed to the goal. Flexibility allows for growth, not by clinging to a failing plan, but by knowing when to pivot.

LIFE WILL TEST YOU, SO ADJUST TO WIN

Here's something that needs to be said: Life doesn't care about plans. Life will throw obstacles at you and test you at the worst possible moments. People talk about planning for success like it's a straight line, but it's actually a messy road full of unexpected twists. And those who make it through aren't the ones with a perfect plan. They're the ones who knew how to adapt when the plan fell apart.

In moments of overwhelm, avoid tunnel vision. The mind will fixate on what's going wrong, and frustration will build. But those moments are when a powerful tool comes into play: Adaptability. Stepping back, assessing the situation from a new angle, and adjusting can turn a setback into an opportunity for growth.

Overcoming challenges is often as simple as shifting focus. Sometimes, it's about changing the way you approach the grind. Just because something worked before doesn't mean that approach will keep working. The most successful people know how to read the room, recognize when it's time to switch things up, and when to double down. Life's tests aren't about breaking you; they're about showing you where you need to adjust. Strength builds from recognizing when to shift gears, when to push harder, and when to pull back.

Reflection

- **Recognize overwhelm**: Write down the last time you felt as though life was slipping out of your control. What happened, and how did it make you feel? What thoughts or actions could you have adjusted to regain focus?
- **Plan your reset**: If overwhelm has persisted in your life, make a plan to reset. Whether you enjoy time off, shift to a new environment, or change your routine, outline steps for a proper recharge.
- **Master the pivot**: Think about a time when an idea didn't go as planned, but adjustments led to a positive outcome. How can that experience help you face future challenges with more confidence?

CHAPTER SEVEN: BUILDING MENTAL TOUGHNESS

PART I: WHAT IS MENTAL TOUGHNESS?

Mental toughness separates people who talk about success from those who actually achieve it. Mental toughness is the grit, resilience, and inner strength that keep you in the game when everything around you is trying to pull you out. There's this belief that success comes from talent or luck, but when life hits you with hardship, mental toughness keeps you moving forward.

THE STRENGTH TO KEEP MOVING FORWARD

People often confuse mental toughness with being invincible, but mental strength is not about pretending that you don't feel pain or pressure. It's about acknowledging your pain and pushing through. Most people only push themselves when things are easy. When life is good, when the sun is shining, it's easy to stay motivated. But what happens when life gets hard? When nothing goes your way? That's when mental toughness shows up.

Building mental toughness is like training a muscle. You don't become stronger by lifting light weights; you become stronger by pushing beyond what's comfortable. And just like physical strength, mental toughness is built over time. Every time you face adversity and refuse to back down, you're building that mental muscle. You're proving to yourself that you can handle whatever life throws at you. Think about the days when everything seemed stacked against you. Maybe it was a financial struggle, personal loss, or professional setback. You're still here! Which means you've built mental toughness. Those challenges became opportunities to grow stronger, and you proved yourself capable.

YOU AREN'T BORN MENTALLY TOUGH

There's a misconception that mental toughness is something people are born with. You hear it all the time. "He's mentally tough" or "She's built different." But here's the truth: Nobody is born with it. Everyone has to earn it. Mental toughness develops over time through experience, struggle, and failure.

Successful people don't achieve greatness by avoiding hardship but because they face challenges, accept their losses, and keep going. That's what mentally tough people do—they use setbacks as fuel to push harder.

I wasn't born mentally tough, but I built this muscle through struggle. Whether sleeping on the floor or dealing with personal loss, life wasn't set up for me to win. But those struggles made me who I am. They built my character and made me resilient. The setbacks and hardships didn't break me. They made me stronger. And that's what mental toughness is—taking the hits and getting back up, time and time again.

MENTAL TOUGHNESS AND GROWTH GO HAND IN HAND

Mental toughness and growth are inseparable. You can't grow unless you push past your limits. Growth happens when you step into discomfort and keep going, even when you want to quit. The problem is most people want to avoid discomfort. They want the results, but they don't want to go through the grind. Mental toughness allows you to embrace discomfort. Mental toughness gives you the strength to keep pushing, but are you willing to go through the pain that comes with the journey? Because that's reality—growth often breeds pain. You don't become stronger by doing what's easy. You become stronger by doing what's hard. Mentally tough people lean into challenges, viewing these obstacles as chances to grow. Your mental toughness will be the driving force that keeps you moving when everything in you is telling you to stop.

THE BATTLE IN YOUR MIND

The toughest battle you'll ever face is the battle of the mind, not outside competition but what's happening in your head. When things get tough, your mind will be your biggest enemy or your best friend.

Your enemy will throw excuses, doubts, and fears at you. It will tell you to quit or take the easy way out.

Enter: Mental toughness.

Mental toughness will quiet those negative voices to help you focus on your goals.

How many times have you told yourself that you'll do it tomorrow or you just don't feel like lifting today?

That's the battle in your head.

That's your mind trying to take the easy way out.

But mentally tough people don't let those thoughts win. They recognize those thoughts as temporary feelings. Winning that battle takes time and practice. It's not about being perfect but remaining consistent. Every time you push past those excuses, you build mental toughness. And the more you do it, the easier it becomes to shut out negativity. Eventually, you will train your mind to focus on the mission, no matter what.

Reflection

- **Assess your mental toughness**: Write down a recent challenge you faced. How did you handle it? Did you push through, or did you let the setback stop you? What can you do differently next time to show more mental toughness?
- **Embrace the struggle**: Think about an area in your life where you've been avoiding discomfort. How can you start embracing discomfort and using it to build mental toughness?

- **Make the daily choice**: Mental toughness is a choice. What's something you can choose to do today to build your mental toughness? How can you commit to making that choice every day?

PART II: STRATEGIES FOR RESILIENCE – TECHNIQUES TO STAY MENTALLY STRONG

Resilience is about how you respond when life throws problems your way. One of the biggest lessons I've learned is that the problem never causes chaos. It's the reaction. People think the challenge is the issue, but in reality, the mess happens because of how we choose to respond. Reacting with anger, frustration, or a bad attitude only makes the problem worse.

Here is where God comes into play. Too often, we're quick to react without realizing that's the exact moment when God is testing us. I've learned that the hardest battles aren't meant to break us but to build us. But if we're too caught up in our emotions that we miss what God is trying to teach us? When things go wrong, your reaction will reflect your faith. Are you trusting the process, or are you letting the pressure make you lose sight of your faith?

THE POWER OF YOUR RESPONSE

Something that stuck with me over the years is the importance of a reaction. I remember being younger, constantly getting into fights because I didn't know how to control my emotions. Someone would say something slick, or I'd be in a situation where I felt disrespected, and my first instinct was to snap. But reacting that way never solved anything. If anything, it made the situation worse.

Over time, I realized I was creating more problems for myself by reacting out of emotion. The situations that could've been handled calmly and logically turned into full-blown messes because I let my emotions take over. And here's the brutal truth: Sometimes, God lets us sit in those messes until we learn the lesson. It took me a long time to realize that my reaction wasn't just about me but whether I was willing to trust God's process.

People want to blame their circumstances, but they rarely take a step back to assess how they responded to the situation or if they could've handled it better. Nine times out of ten, their reaction played a bigger role in the outcome than the situation itself.

CONTROLLING YOUR REACTION

Controlling your emotions doesn't mean you ignore how you're feeling, but it does mean learning to pause before reacting. When something doesn't go as planned, take a breath instead of flying off the handle or letting frustration get the best of you. That pause is where you need to let God work. Moments of stillness should remind you that no matter how chaotic things seem, God's got you. He's working behind the scenes, but you must give Him space to move.

It's easy to react with frustration when you're hit with setbacks, but what does that really solve?

Nothing.

In fact, it usually makes things worse.

People often think resilience means being unaffected by stress or pressure, but true resilience is feeling those emotions without letting them take control. Whether it's a business deal that has gone wrong or a personal issue, reacting emotionally fuels the fire. But when you train yourself to pause, step back, and assess the situation, you realize that most problems aren't as bad as they seem. Even if they are, reacting with a calm, focused mind and faith gives you a better chance of solving them.

HOW I LEARNED TO CONTROL MY REACTIONS

One of my hardest moments was while I was still figuring out my path, trying to make a name for myself, and dealing with the setbacks that come with the grind. There were days when I felt like everything was stacked against me, and the temptation to react with anger or frustration was strong. During this time, I had just lost a few clients, and some business deals fell through, too. It felt like all the progress I had made was being ripped out from under me. My initial reaction was frustration. I remember thinking, "Why is this happening to me? What did I do wrong?"

That's when I had to check myself.

Frustration wasn't going to fix anything. Instead of reacting emotionally, I took a step back to reflect. I prayed on it, asking God for clarity and patience. That pause gave me the space to look at the situation differently. I figured out where I went wrong, what I could've done better, and how to move forward.

And here's where faith came in—I had to believe that God was testing me for my good. He wasn't punishing me. He was preparing me. But if I had reacted poorly, I would've missed the lesson. Breakthroughs often come right after setbacks, but only if you're willing to see the situation through God's eyes.

PRACTICAL TECHNIQUES FOR BUILDING RESILIENCE

So, how do you build resilience? How do you train yourself to react soundly in tough situations? Here are key techniques to keep you mentally strong:

1. **The power of the pause**. The first step is learning to pause. When something goes wrong, take a breath. Don't react immediately. Give yourself a moment to assess the situation. In that pause, remember that God is working for you, not against you. Taking a brief pause will be the difference between reacting emotionally and responding with faith.
2. **Mindset shift.** Instead of processing setbacks as failures, look at them as opportunities to grow. Every challenge holds a lesson, and often, it's God's way of guiding you to grow. When you shift your mindset from "why is this happening to me" to "what is God trying to show me," you start to see obstacles as part of a bigger plan.
3. **Reflect**. After every setback, take time to reflect. What went wrong? How did you handle the situation? What could you have done differently? Reflection isn't just about learning from the past. It's

about seeing how God is guiding you through every challenge and preparing you for what's next.
4. **Positive self-talk.** The voice in your head can be your biggest supporter or your worst enemy. When life gets tough, pay attention to how you talk to yourself. Are you building yourself up or tearing yourself down? Resilient people use positive self-talk to stay focused, knowing that with God's strength, they can handle anything.

BRUTAL HONESTY: IT'S ON YOU

Here's the brutal truth: No one will make you resilient. No one will teach you how to control your emotions. That's something you must take responsibility for. God can guide you, but you have to choose to follow His guidance. It's easy to place blame, but at the end of the day, the only thing you have control over is yourself and your faith. It's on you to decide how to respond when life hits you with challenges. You can let those challenges break you, or you can use them to build you. And here's the part most people don't want to hear: God won't hand you results. You must work for them. But the good news is, if you trust the process, God will provide everything you need.

PART III: TURNING PAIN INTO POWER

Pain is inevitable, but what separates the people who break from those who rise above it is the ability to take their pain and turn it into power. The darkest moments in your life will shape you, but you must decide how your pain will take shape. I'm not just referring to small pains. I'm talking about the kind of pain that leaves you broken, the kind that makes you question everything, even your existence. I've been through that kind of pain. And I had to make a choice to stay broken or turn that pain into something that could fuel me for the rest of my life.

THE SUICIDE ATTEMPT

Thoughts about unaliving myself started at 12 years old. Most people don't expect a 12-year-old to deal with depression or suicidal thoughts, but that was my reality. I felt like I was drowning in fear that I wasn't enough. No matter what I did, I felt like I didn't belong and was always on the outside looking in. For a 12-year-old, my concerns felt heavy. Comparison was poison to my mind. But at 12 years old, I didn't have the tools to deal with deep feelings or societal pressure. So, I remained trapped in a life where I felt unworthy, unseen, and unable to imagine a future worth looking forward to.

With a thank-you letter set aside for my parents, explaining that my decision to end it all wasn't their fault, I sat in my room with a knife in my hand, ready to say goodbye.

I still remember the weight of that moment. But as soon as I heard my mom call my name from the kitchen, her voice somehow snapped me out of it.

It wasn't the end, and it wasn't my time to go. That moment became a turning point for me, even though I didn't fully understand the gravity of this shift.

It's crazy to think that at 12 years old, I was ready to leave this world, but life is often understood backward. Looking back, that was just the beginning of my story. That moment became the first step toward uncovering my purpose, although it took years of reflection and growth to understand. Pain can destroy you if you let it, but it can also become the foundation for greatness.

A CONVERSATION WITH MY YOUNGER SELF

That boy sitting in his room, holding a knife, ready to end it all, he couldn't see past the pain. He thought those feelings wouldn't stop, that the embarrassment, struggles, and feelings of inadequacy would last forever. He thought there was no future worth living for.

But he was wrong.

I look at my life now, the impact I'm making, the people I'm helping, and the way I carry myself with purpose and discipline, and I see a young version of myself staring back, the one who felt like he didn't matter. And I talk to him. I tell him everything he needed to hear back then.

"I see you. I hear you. And life gets better."

I tell him that every fight, tear, and sleepless night was not in vain. I remind him that every time he felt like he wasn't enough, that he was being prepared for something greater, that all of those moments of pain and doubt were steppingstones toward a future he couldn't imagine at the time.

You didn't go through all of that for nothing.

I'm proud of you.

We spend a lot of time healing from what other people did to us, but we don't spend enough time healing the relationship we have with ourselves. We don't take enough time to sit with our younger selves and say, "I'm sorry for what I put you through. I'm sorry for not believing in you. I'm sorry for trying to hide you, run from you, and act like you didn't matter."

But healing doesn't happen by ignoring the past. Healing happens when you acknowledge the past, learn from it, and choose to show up differently.

Now, every action I take is a way to honor the child who almost didn't make it. When I wake up early and push myself to be better, I do it for him. When I train athletes, step on a stage to speak, or pour into others, I do it for him. Because he fought to survive, and now I owe it to him to live, and not just exist but truly live.

If you're reading this, I want you to take a second and think about the younger version of yourself, the one who was scared and lost and wanted to feel like they mattered. Now ask yourself if you're living in a way that makes them proud. Are you taking care of them? Because they're still in you, waiting for you to acknowledge them.

You don't have to keep carrying the pain of your past. You don't have to be a prisoner to what happened to you. You have the power to rewrite your story and create a life that the younger version of you could've only dreamed of.

THE LOSS OF MY FATHER

The death of my father was yet another life-testing situation. Losing him felt like the ground had been ripped out from under me. My father was my anchor, the person I looked up to, the man who taught me to box and who worked hard to provide for us. When he passed away, I felt like a part of me died with him.

I'll never forget the day he passed. I was going about my day when I got a call from my sister, telling me to come home immediately. Something in her voice made my heart drop. I rushed home, and when I got there, I saw my dad lying lifeless on the floor.

I froze, just staring at him, and everything went blank. The pain hit harder than anything I've ever felt.

I dropped to the floor, directly next to him, crying, "Dad, I'm sorry…," but no matter how much I cried, he never replied.

And it tore me apart knowing that our last conversation was an argument about something as stupid as car insurance. I didn't get to tell him I loved him one last time. That moment haunts me to this day, the fact that I never got to say goodbye or that he couldn't hear me apologize.

There's no way to describe the emptiness that comes with losing a parent. Parental loss is a different kind of pain, one that sits in your chest and doesn't go away. My father wasn't just a provider. He represented resilience. He showed me that no matter how hard life gets, you keep pushing. But when he died, those lessons seemed meaningless. I began floating in a space of confusion, anger, and sadness. The pain I felt was the type that knocks you completely off course.

But here's what I learned through the loss of my father: Pain doesn't have to be permanent. Yes, pain stays with you, but it doesn't have to control you. My dad's death shook me to my core, but it also ignited something within. Losing my father made me realize that I had a responsibility, not just to myself, but to his legacy. I couldn't let his hard work and sacrifices go to waste. I had a new fire within, one that made me hungry to succeed and honor him by becoming the man I knew I was capable of being.

Turning pain into power doesn't mean the pain disappears. It means you find a way to use it and to let it drive you instead of destroying you. My father's death pushed me to a new level. His passing forced me to dig deep and find strength I didn't know existed. When I think about giving up, I think of my father. I remember everything he did for me, and his memory keeps me going.

FINDING STRENGTH IN THE STRUGGLE

Whether it's the loss of a loved one, a failed relationship, financial struggles, or mental health battles, pain is universal, but it's not the end of your life unless you let it. You have two choices when you're faced with pain: Let it consume you or use it to propel you.

People always ask me how I stay motivated and push through setbacks. The answer is simple: I learned how to turn my pain into power. I took the darkest moments of my life—the suicide attempt, the loss of my father, financial struggles, and the feeling of being stuck—and I use them as fuel.

But turning pain into power isn't about pretending the pain doesn't exist. It's about acknowledging it, sitting with it, and deciding to move forward. It's about saying, "Yes, this hurts, and yes, this is hard, but I'm not going to let this break me."

Finding strength in struggle is not about having all the answers but about believing that the struggle is shaping you for something greater. Strength builds when you hit rock bottom and climb your way back up. Every climb makes you stronger. Every setback prepares you for a comeback. The deeper the pain, the deeper your capacity for growth. The struggle refines you like gold being purified in the fire. It burns, but on the other side of that heat, you'll find a stronger, more resilient version of yourself.

When I look back at my darkest moments, I know that my pain was actually a gift. It gave me an edge, a strength that can't be taught. If I hadn't gone through those struggles, I wouldn't be the person I am today. I wouldn't have the same hunger to succeed or a relentless drive to keep going. If you can find strength in the struggle, nothing can stop you because every challenge becomes another opportunity to rise.

BRUTAL HONESTY: PAIN IS THE PRICE OF GROWTH

If you're serious about becoming the best version of yourself and achieving greatness, you have to go through the fire. You can't avoid it. The pain you feel today will prepare you for the success you'll have tomorrow, but only if you let it.

The truth is nobody wants to hear that pain is necessary. In a world where instant gratification is king, people want rewards without work and glory without the grind. But that's not how life works. Pain is the prerequisite for growth. Whether it's physical pain from pushing your body to the limit or emotional pain from dealing with loss, it's all part of the journey. And here's the kicker: The more you avoid the pain, the longer you delay your growth.

Think about it. Every time you've truly leveled up in life, it's been after a period of struggle. It's the setbacks that teach you the most and show you what you're really made of. People who reach their goals are willing to endure the pain, embrace it, and keep going even when it feels impossible. They understand that the pain isn't there to destroy them but to build them.

Here's the thing: Pain won't last forever, but the strength you gain from it will. That's why you have to stop running from it. You have to stop looking for the easy way out because there isn't one. The only way to grow is to go through the fire.

Reflection
- **Face the pain**: Think about a moment in your life when you experienced deep pain. How did you respond? Did you let it break you, or did you find a way to move forward? What did that pain teach you, and how can you use it to fuel your growth?
- **Honor your struggle(s)**: Reflect on a time when you felt lost or broken. What strength did you find in that moment? How can you honor that struggle by using it to push you toward your goals?
- **Turn pain into power**: Write down the areas in your life where you're still carrying pain. How can you turn that pain into power?

What steps can you take today to use that pain as fuel for your future?

PART IV: OVERCOMING THE BRICK WALL – PUSHING THROUGH WHEN YOU WANT TO QUIT

At some point, everybody hits a wall. You can grind for years, put in the work, and do all the right things and still hit a point when it feels like progress has stalled, and you're unsure of what comes next. Most people see a wall and think it's the end. They look at it and immediately start making excuses: "Maybe I'm not built for this," or "Maybe this isn't for me." But the wall isn't there to stop you; it's there to see how much you're willing to break through it.

And here's the real challenge: It's not even about the grind anymore. This is a different battle. This is you vs. your own doubt. When you hit a wall, and everything feels like it's at a standstill, your mind will start feeding you lies:

Maybe you've gone as far as you can.

Maybe you should quit.

That's a mental war right there.

But let's get real about the wall. The wall isn't telling you to stop. It's merely a checkpoint. Most people hit that wall and think they've reached their limit. But the wall is just testing how bad you really want it. It's separating the ones who are all talk from the ones who are actually about this life. It's asking, "Will you keep showing up when it feels like you're not making progress?"

Real talk, most people aren't built for the long game. Everybody loves the start. They're hyped, motivated, and ready to roll. But when they hit a wall and the excitement fades, they fold, not because they're weak but because they haven't built the mindset for long-term success. The wall doesn't mean stop; it means you're close to something big. When you're pushing against that wall, even if it's not moving, every push makes you stronger.

WHY YOU CAN'T LET FEAR WIN

Here's the thing: Fear leads people to quit. People typically don't quit because they're lazy or weak but because fear gets in their heads. Fear of failing, fear of looking stupid, and fear of not being enough starts creeping in when progress slows down. But here's the reality: Fear is just an illusion. It's your mind playing tricks on you, making the wall seem bigger than it is. Most of the time, the wall isn't even a real obstacle but your own self-doubt. That voice is a liar. You can do it, and the only thing that will stop you is if you give in to that fear.

The only real failure is quitting. As long as you're still moving, you're still in the game. But the second you let fear win and decide to stop is when you've failed. Fear is a natural part of life, but you can't let it control you. You have to recognize it for what it is—a feeling, not a fact—and keep moving.

Fear only has power if you feed it. Fear will whisper in your ear, "What if you fail? What if this doesn't work?" But those "what ifs" don't matter. What matters is that you keep going. Every time you push through fear, you weaken it. And the more you push through, the stronger you become and the more confident you feel. Fear will lose its grip on you, and your confidence will carry you to the next level.

CHAPTER EIGHT: THE FOUNDATION OF SELF-DISCIPLINE

PART I: WHY DISCIPLINE IS THE BACKBONE OF SUCCESS

EXERCISING DISCIPLINE DURING MY LOWEST POINT

After my father passed away, I found myself living in an unfinished basement. It was cold and damp, and I felt like I hit rock bottom. I was drowning in financial stress, with my bank account in the negative. Every day, I'd get hit with overdraft fees, and it got to the point where I had to call the bank and beg them to stop charging me. It was humiliating.

The discipline to keep showing up saved me. Every day, I woke up with a plan to claw my way out of that hole. I had to find a way to make money, grind harder than ever, and never end up in this situation again. It wasn't about motivation because, believe me, there were no motivational speeches in that basement. It was about pure discipline, showing up every day, even when everything in me wanted to give up. I realized that discipline isn't something you tap into when life is going well; it's what carries you through when life feels unbearable.

You Don't Rise to the Occasion.
You Fall to Your Level of Discipline.

When life gets hard, you don't suddenly rise to the occasion. You fall to the level of your discipline. That's why discipline has to be something you build consistently. Because when the challenges come—and they will come—your discipline will carry you through.

Discipline is about who you are when no one's watching. It's about what you do when nobody is there to hold you accountable. It's the choices you make in the quiet moments when it's just you and your goals. Those choices add up. Over time, they build a foundation that success can stand on.

Reflection
- **Where are you lacking discipline?** Identify one area in your life where you're consistently falling short because of a lack of discipline.
- **What promises have you broken to yourself?** Write down three times you've told yourself you'd do something and didn't follow through.
- **What's one non-negotiable you can commit to today?** Make one small commitment to yourself, something you will do every day, no matter what.

PART II: STEPS FOR BUILDING DISCIPLINE

You build discipline by making intentional choices every day, no matter how small those decisions seem. You don't wake up one day and suddenly have all the discipline in the world. It starts with small wins. Think of it like laying bricks. You don't build a house in one day, but if you lay one brick at a time, you will eventually have a strong foundation. Discipline is no different. You can't fake it, and you can't skip steps. The only way to develop it is through action. Here's how to start:

1. Start with small wins. Here's where most people go wrong. They think they need to overhaul their entire life overnight. That's why they fail. You don't need to change everything at once. You just need to secure one small win today. When you rack up small wins, they add up to big victories over time.

Let's say you've been struggling to wake up early. Don't start by trying to wake up at 4 AM every day when you've been hitting snooze until 9. Start by waking up 30 minutes earlier. That's it, just 30 minutes. Win that small battle.

But most people bite off more than they can chew, get overwhelmed, and quit before they get started. But what they don't realize is that starting small makes the process manageable. It's easier to commit to something small, and when you start seeing those small wins stack up, it builds confidence. And confidence will help you take on bigger challenges down the line.

That's how discipline is built.

You show yourself that you can win small battles, and once you do that, you gain the confidence to tackle bigger challenges. Small wins create momentum. And momentum is everything when you're building discipline. Once you have that momentum, you can start applying that discipline to bigger areas of your life, whether it's your fitness goals, your career, or your mindset. But be sure to start small.

For example, when I was clawing my way out of that basement, I didn't start by trying to fix everything at once. I focused on getting small wins. If I could get up at 4 AM and knock out my workout, that would be a win. If I could train one client each day, that would be a win. Those small wins gave me the energy to keep going. Over time, they accumulated, and that's what helped me dig myself out of that hole. It wasn't one big move, but a series of small wins stacked up over time.

2. Create Non-Negotiables: Here's a key to discipline that most people overlook – You have to set non-negotiables. Non-negotiables are commitments you refuse to break. It doesn't matter how tired or stressed you are, because when you create non-negotiables, you take the decision-making process out of the equation. It's not about waking up and asking yourself, "Do I feel like doing this today?" It's about waking up and knowing that this is what you'll do.

This is another area where many people fail. They treat their goals like options or activities they'll get to if they feel like it. But discipline isn't about convenience. It's about following through regardless of feelings. Your non-negotiables are the foundation of your discipline. They set the tone for everything else in your life.

My non-negotiables are waking up early, working out every day, and constantly leveling up my mindset. These happen no matter what. It doesn't matter if I'm tired or stressed. These are my non-negotiable because they set the standard for my productivity, energy, and overall success. When I keep these in check, everything else—my business, relationships, ability to lead, and long-term goals—falls into place.

When you establish your non-negotiables, you remove the guesswork from your day. You don't have to think about whether you'll work out. Instead, you just do it because that's part of who you are. You become the person who doesn't negotiate with yourself. And when you stop negotiating, change becomes inevitable.

Action step: Write down three non-negotiables for your life. These could be as simple as drinking a gallon of water, spending 30 minutes reading, or working out for 30 minutes. The key is to commit, regardless of circumstances. Once you set your non-negotiables, believe that they'll become a part of who you are.

3. Eliminate distractions. If you're serious about building discipline, you must eliminate distractions. Distractions are silent killers of discipline. Every time you let something pull your attention away from what you're supposed to be doing, you weaken your ability to stay disciplined. The more distractions you allow, the harder it becomes to stick to your goals.

We live in a world full of distractions. Social media, Netflix, and notifications, they're all designed to keep you from focusing on what matters. Every time you pick up your phone and start scrolling, you feed a habit that destroys your discipline. You might not notice it at first, but over time, those distractions add up, and suddenly, you're spending more time avoiding your goals than working toward them.

The worst part? Distractions become habits, and every time you give in, you make it harder on yourself to focus. That's why you have to be ruthless about eliminating distractions.

Action step: Identify your biggest distractions. What's pulling you away from your goals? Is it social media, television, staying up too late, or hanging around the wrong people? Cut out those distractions. If that means deleting apps from your phone, do it. If it means setting time limits for certain activities, do that. If you're serious about leveling up, you must be willing to cut out anything that's slowing you down.

Once you start removing distractions, you'll notice how much more focused and productive you become. You'll have more mental energy to put toward your goals. This level of change might be uncomfortable at first—because distractions are addictive—but the payoff will be huge. You'll be more present, more intentional, and more disciplined.

4. Be consistent, even when you fail. Failure is a part of life, but the good news is that discipline isn't about being perfect. It's about being consistent. When you fail, the key is not to stay down but to get up, show up, and keep going. A lot of people think that once they slip up, it's game over. They miss one workout, or they eat something unhealthy, and suddenly, they believe they've ruined everything. But here's the truth: Failure isn't the end. It's just part of the journey, a reminder that progress is built on persistence, not perfection.

Consistency is the difference maker. Anybody can be disciplined for a day, a week, or a month, but real discipline is about what you do long term. It's about showing up after you've fallen off. Discipline is the ability to push forward no matter how many times you stumble.

In the beginning, the process of building discipline will be messy. You'll slip up. You'll have days when you don't stick to your plan. But those aren't excuses to quit. The real test is how fast you can recover. Can you miss a day and come back stronger? Can you fail but keep going?

Reflection
- **What's one small win you can commit to today?** Start with something simple that you can execute immediately.
- **What are your daily non-negotiables?** Write down three things that you will commit to doing every day.
- **What distractions are holding you back?** Be honest with yourself about the distractions that are keeping you from your goals and commit to cutting them out.
- **How will you handle failure?** Think about how you've responded to failure in the past. What will you do differently next time?

PART III: BENEFITS OF LIVING A DISCIPLINED LIFE

Here's what many people want to know: *What do I get from all this hard work?*

When you commit to living a disciplined life, you're not just grinding for the sake of grinding. Every bit of effort you put in comes back to you in ways that go beyond hitting a goal. Discipline changes how you see yourself, how others see you, and the level of success you're able to reach. Here are the rewards you can expect when you commit to a life of discipline:

1. Control over your life. One of the first rewards you gain from discipline is control. Most people don't realize how much control they've given away. They're controlled by impulses, emotions, habits, and others' expectations. When you build discipline, you take back that control. You stop reacting to life and start living on your own terms.

When you're disciplined, you make decisions based on what's best for you, not based on temporary feelings or distractions. You start living intentionally instead of letting life happen to you. When you're disciplined, you're not easily swayed by others' opinions, peer pressure, or fear of missing out. You're grounded in what you need to do, and that's powerful.

A lot of my depression came from not realizing how much control I was giving away. I'd react to everything – people's opinions, circumstances I couldn't change, and situations that didn't serve me. It was all wasted energy. The more I focused on what I couldn't control, the more anxious and frustrated I became. But when I started locking in on what I could control—my actions, my reactions, and my effort—my anxiety began to lift. This brings peace, and peace brings joy. Discipline isn't just about achieving your goals but freeing yourself from everything that doesn't matter.

2. Confidence and self-respect. Discipline builds confidence. Every time you do what you said you would do, you build trust with yourself. That trust turns into confidence because you know you can rely on yourself. When you lack confidence, it's easy to get lost in comparison. And comparison is the thief of joy. The Bible tells us that.

But when you're disciplined, you're building confidence and self-respect every day. You're no longer worried about who's doing what because you're focused on your journey and growth. Confidence doesn't just make you feel good; it increases your self-knowledge. You start to understand who you are, what you're capable of, and who you can become.

My confidence didn't come overnight. It came from consistently doing what I said I'd do, from proving to myself, day in and day out, that I'm the type of person who gets things done. And when you have that level of self-respect, it changes how you move, think, and see yourself.

3. Respect. People respect discipline. Even if they don't say it out loud, they notice. When you're disciplined, people see you as reliable, consistent, and committed. You become someone they can count on, someone they know will show up and deliver.

Successful people respect discipline because they know how much it takes to win. How am I, in my late 20s, going from poverty and living in an unfinished basement, to giving advice to millionaires?

Because they respect my daily discipline.

They see my hustle, grind, and commitment to my goals.

That respect isn't about money or status but in the way I show up every day. Even if they're more successful, my work ethic is easily acknowledged, and that earns me a seat at the table. They see that I live what I preach, and that's rare. Discipline builds credibility, and credibility builds connections. It's not just about achieving personal success; it's about earning the respect and trust of others around you.

And that respect can lead to opportunities you'd never have if you were relying on talent alone.

4. Success in every area of your life. Discipline isn't about crushing one goal. It's the foundation for success in every area of your life. Whether it's your career, health, relationships, or personal growth, discipline is the thread that ties everything together. When you're disciplined, you're more likely to stick to your workout plan, stay focused at work, and show up consistently for the people who matter to you.

Most people don't realize that the same discipline that helps you in one area can be applied everywhere. If you can stay disciplined in the gym, you can stay disciplined at work. If you can commit to learning something new every day, that discipline will benefit your career, mindset, and relationships.

Discipline compounds.

Every time you show up in one area, it strengthens your ability to show up in another.

I didn't become disciplined just by working out. I took that discipline and applied it to my business, personal development, and relationships. It wasn't just about achieving one goal; it was about becoming the type of person who can achieve any goal.

5. Freedom through structure. This might sound ironic, but discipline gives you freedom. Most people think of discipline as restrictive, but the truth is that it frees you from chaos, anxiety, and struggle. When you have discipline, you have a plan, and when you have a plan, you don't waste time or energy on areas of unimportance. Think about it. When you're disciplined, you know exactly what you need to do each day. You're not wasting time being indecisive or letting distractions pull you off track. You're focused, clear-headed, and free from the stress that comes from a lack of direction. You're free to be productive and move toward your goals without second-guessing yourself.

Discipline creates structure, and structure creates freedom. I don't have to guess what I'm supposed to do each day because I've already set my priorities. That's the freedom of discipline. It frees you from the chaos of indecision.

THE HEART OF DISCIPLINE

Let me start by saying that I'm not here to brag. I'm a human being, like you, trying to figure it all out. I'm someone who's made mistakes, learned hard lessons, and faced struggles I didn't think I'd survive. I want you to know that this journey, this path of discipline, isn't about becoming perfect. I'm not perfect, and I don't want you to feel like you have to be, either. I'm here to keep it real with you because that's how I got to where I am—by being brutally honest with myself, embracing vulnerability, and striving for genuine connections. Discipline is a tool, a pathway to something better, but it doesn't make you flawless. It makes you stronger, more aware, and more in control of your life, but above all, the most authentic version of yourself, one that isn't held back by fear, excuses, or distractions.

Discipline has been the answer to a lot of problems I've faced, and I believe it can be the answer to yours, too. When I became serious about discipline, it cleared out toxic environments, late nights at parties where nothing productive was happening, and street corners where people were gossiping and wasting potential. It pushed out toxic people, the ones who laughed at my dreams, only hit me up when they needed something, and didn't respect my time or vision. Discipline forced me to confront harmful habits like procrastination, overindulging in distractions, and spending money recklessly instead of investing. Most importantly, discipline helped me separate myself from people who weren't pouring into my growth, the ones who only wanted to be in my space because of what I could do for them but never challenged me to be better. I had to realize that being surrounded by people doesn't mean you're supported. And if you're the only one giving in every relationship, you're not in a real circle; you're just an energy source for people who don't pour back into you.

Discipline isn't magic, and it's not a quick fix. It takes work, patience, and self-reflection. But I want you to know it won't make you robotic or strip away your personality. You'll become a better version of yourself, someone who makes mistakes but learns from them, who still struggles but pushes through, who still feels but learns to manage emotions with strength.

Look, I'm still growing, still learning, and still falling on my face. I've made a ton of mistakes and will make more. I've gone through lows that pushed me to the edge, moments when I questioned my entire life. I'm not writing this because I've arrived at some destination of perfection and now look down on everyone else. I'm writing this because I know what it's like to feel lost, overwhelmed, and frustrated. I know what it's like to want something better but feel trapped by patterns, habits, and fears.

Don't read this book expecting to walk away as the most disciplined person in the world. Don't think that by following every word, you'll instantly become the most successful, put-together, productive person on Earth. I don't want that for you, anyway. What I want is for you to walk away as a better version of yourself, a more honest, resilient, and compassionate version. I want you to read these words and feel a sense of purpose that drives you to start your journey of growth at your own pace.

The fact that you're reading this tells me you're ready for something more. You want to be better. You want to grow, to let go of whatever's been holding you back, and to step into a version of yourself that you can be proud of. There's a reason you picked up this book, and that was not a coincidence. You're here because you're ready for change, and that's the first step. Discipline is your path forward, but the most important step is being honest with yourself. Look in the mirror and acknowledge where you are right now. Accept this truth without judgment, and from that place of acceptance, start your journey.

Take it one day at a time, one step at a time. Be patient with yourself. There's no finish line in the marathon of achieving discipline. It's a lifelong pursuit, something you build day by day, mistake by mistake. Let this be your start. Don't be afraid to stumble, struggle, or fail. Keep going, and when you feel like giving up, remember why you started.

If you ever need a reminder that someone's got your back, hit me up. Reach out to me on social media, share your journey, challenges, and victories. I'm here not just as an author but as someone who genuinely cares about your growth. I want you to win, succeed, and live a life that makes you proud. So, use this book as a tool. I want nothing less than to see you become the best version of yourself. We're in this together. Let's make it happen.

PART IV: THE REAL COST OF SACRIFICE

When it comes to building a disciplined life, most people talk about the grind and what it takes to succeed. But what doesn't get enough attention is the cost of that journey. Sacrifice isn't just a word; it's a lifestyle. And to get where you want to go, you must be willing to pay the price. When you choose discipline, you often choose a path that requires more than hard work and focus. It demands personal sacrifices that can affect your relationships and social life.

1. The isolation that comes with discipline. One of the toughest realities of discipline is the loneliness that can come with it. When you commit to a disciplined life, you're choosing a path that not everyone will walk with you. Friends and family may not fully understand the drive behind your decisions. Choosing discipline means sacrificing occasional social time and forgoing activities that used to be fun but now feel like distractions. There will be times when you feel isolated and misunderstood.

People often view change as a threat. Jay-Z said it best: "People look at you strange saying you changed, like you worked that hard to stay the same." Those words hit deep because change is the goal here. Yes, I changed, and I take pride in that. When people around you don't understand your growth, they might label it as a negative thing. But understand that change is proof of progress, of becoming who you're meant to be. Not everyone will support that, and discipline might leave you with fewer people in your corner. But the people who are meant to stay will stay. Embrace change and let isolation shape your strength.

2. The sacrifice of time and energy. The biggest sacrifices in the journey to discipline aren't just material; they're your time and energy. Discipline demands a level of commitment that's all-consuming. You're no longer investing in temporary pleasures like binge-watching television every day, spending money on items that don't serve your future, sleeping in when you should be working, or mindlessly scrolling on social media. Instead, you're investing in long-term success, and that requires a relentless work ethic. For me, it meant putting hours into training sessions, staying focused when everyone else was taking breaks, and showing up on days when motivation was nowhere to be found.

There were countless nights when I trained alone, sacrificing sleep and time with friends and family because I held on tightly to what I was working toward. Time is a currency you never get back, and where you spend it matters. Sustaining this level of discipline was hard at first, knowing that I was missing out on moments that everyone else was enjoying. But success isn't built on comfort; it's built on discipline. I poured my energy into the future I wanted, even if that meant letting go of anything that brought me comfort in the present.

3. The emotional toll of sacrifice: Sacrifice often takes an emotional toll. The path to discipline can be emotionally draining, filled with doubt, frustration, and moments when the weight of your choices feels too heavy to carry. There were nights when I questioned everything, when I felt like I was working endlessly but seeing little return on my sacrifices. That kind of emotional exhaustion is something you must confront head-on.

Discipline requires resilience and the ability to find value in every step, even when the journey feels like it's dragging you down. The emotional toll is a part of the price of success, but if you keep your eyes on the purpose behind the pain, you'll have more fuel for the journey.

4. Facing the consequences of your choices: Every sacrifice comes with a consequence. Pursuing your goals often means giving up certain aspects of life that are meaningful, like time with family or moments that can't be relived. For example, after moving to Orlando, I missed out on spending holidays with my mom and sister because I had client sessions, was working on my brand, and catching up to complete online work. Knowing they were celebrating without me hurt, but I knew I was building something that would make the future better for all of us.

That's a hard reality to accept, that achieving your dreams often means putting distance between you and the people you love or missing out on moments you can't get back. But remember that sacrifice isn't forever but a temporary cost to secure a lasting reward. Missing those holidays wasn't easy, but I focused on the future I was working toward, a future where my sacrifices would pay off for the people I care about. Success asks for trade-offs, and you must decide if temporary sacrifices are worth the legacy you're building. For me, the answer was always yes.

5. Staying strong when sacrifice tests you: One of the hardest things about sacrifice is resisting the urge to quit. The truth is that sacrifice and struggle are parts of greatness, and nothing worth having comes easy. I remember sitting in my car one night, completely drained, staring at my bank account that was in the negative. I asked myself how I got to this point. Bills were piling up, my Jeep just broke down, and I felt like no matter how hard I worked, I was barely treading water. I had just finished a long day of training clients, my body was exhausted, and my mind was even worse. I sat there gripping the steering wheel, wondering, "Why am I even doing this? Is this grind even paying off?" Everything in me wanted to stop, to take the easy route and go back to something comfortable, but deep down, I knew quitting wouldn't solve anything; it would just delay my success.

Choosing to keep going when every part of you wants to give up is a test of strength. I've always said, "Choose your hard." Being average is hard, and being great is hard. But if I have to pick, I'll go out with my shield and fight for greatness. I know what average looks like because I've lived it. I've seen what life is like on that side: poverty, disappointment, and unfulfilled potential.

I refuse to go back.

I want to see success, wealth, and freedom for my family. I want to taste greatness before I settle for anything less. That's what pushes me when the sacrifice feels too heavy, and I hope it pushes you, too. Remember why you're fighting and know that hard moments are merely a part of the journey to living your potential.

THE HEART OF SACRIFICE

Let me be real with you. Sacrifice is hard, and it's not something you'll always feel strong enough to carry. It's easy to talk about sacrifice, but when you're in it and making choices that pull you away from comfort, security, and familiarity, it feels like an uphill battle. But I'm here to tell you it's a battle worth fighting. This journey isn't just about reaching a destination; it's about building resilience, discovering what you're truly capable of, and proving to yourself that you have the strength to push through.

I didn't start out strong. I wasn't always the person who could carry this weight and give up things I loved for something I couldn't see. But discipline, sacrifice, and a deep sense of purpose transformed me. I look back and see everything I gave up—time with friends, moments of comfort, easy days—and I see the strength those sacrifices gave me in return. The person I am today was built by every choice I made to keep going, pushing, and sacrificing.

Sacrifice doesn't make you better than anyone, but it does make you better than the version of yourself who was okay with staying the same. This isn't about achieving a perfect vision of success. It's about becoming a person who can handle whatever life throws at them, a person who's resilient, tough, and focused.

So here's my message to you: Sacrifice isn't just about letting go; it's about choosing to invest in yourself, your future, and the life you deserve. The road will get hard, and you'll face moments when giving up feels like the best option. But remember that you're not sacrificing for the sake of sacrifice; you're building the life you're meant to live. Hold on to your "why," and let that keep you grounded. Sacrifice will shape you, and discipline will strengthen you. In the end, you'll find yourself on the other side, stronger, wiser, and more in control of your life than you ever imagined.

I want you to understand this because it took me too long to see it myself. When I look back, I see that every struggle, every step forward, every "small" win was molding the life I wanted. I don't want you to miss out on that realization, so celebrate the journey, respect the process, and remember that roadblocks make you stronger. Just by reading this book, you're progressing, so let each win remind you of what you're capable of.

CHAPTER NINE: RADICAL ACCOUNTABILITY

PART I: TAKING FULL RESPONSIBILITY

In the game of life, each of us is dealt a hand of cards at birth, cards we didn't choose. Some of us are born into poverty, others into broken homes, and some with odds stacked against them. These cards are our starting point, but they don't define the outcome. Our role is to take full responsibility for how we play our hand. You can't swap out your cards, and you can't avoid the game, but you are able to decide how you approach every day. There are key principles that separate those who make the most of their circumstances from those who stay stuck. Here are pertinent rules to playing your hand wisely.

Rule #1: Accept the cards in your hand: This first rule is simple. There's no point in comparing your hand to someone else's, wishing your hand was different, or blaming circumstances for what you don't have. Your hand is your hand. Just like no one sits down to play Uno and hopes for a losing hand, you have to pick up your cards and start strategizing with what's in front of you. Every card, every challenge, can be played in a way that helps you move forward. It's on you to choose how you play, and that's a key step to winning.

Everyone's got a tough hand in some way. Maybe you're short but dream of making it big in sports. Athletes like Muggsy Bogues, Nate Robinson, and Isaiah Thomas faced that same card and found a way to the top. Maybe you were born into poverty but want to be rich. Oprah Winfrey, Steve Harvey, J.K. Rowling, and Kevin Hart held that card and turned it into a win. Or maybe you're born with a rare disorder and want a fulfilling life. People like Nick Vujicic and Helen Keller took that card and made it work. Taking responsibility means choosing to play your cards with intention and eliminating excuses about why it "can't be done." Because once you're in the game, nobody cares how rough your hand is. They only see how you play it.

Rule #2: Cut the excuses and play to win: In life, just like in any game, the goal is to win. That doesn't mean "winning" in comparison to others but winning against the obstacles you're facing to reach your full potential. Playing to win means looking at every obstacle and asking, "How can I use this to push me forward?" The second you allow excuses to enter the game, you're choosing to play for a loss. Excuses keep you stuck, but responsibility keeps you moving.

Owning your choices and taking control of your actions is the ultimate power move. People love to blame their past, environment, and circumstances, but the fact is, you have control over your next move. That's where radical accountability comes in. Stop focusing on obstacles and start focusing on how you'll win with what you've got.

Rule #3: Find your cheat code. When I was a kid, I played GTA and Madden, and I'd look up cheat codes to make the experience even better or to win the level. Life is no different. Every day comes with its own cheat code if you're willing to look for it. Finding your cheat code is about discovering the small things you can do to set yourself up for a daily win. It's like finding your unique boost, something that elevates your mindset, improves your day, and keeps you on track.

Maybe your cheat code is starting the day with a workout, and that sets the tone, gives you energy, and keeps you in a positive mindset all day long. Maybe it's going for a walk and talking to God, grounding yourself before you dive into your responsibilities. That's your cheat code for the day, a healthy, intentional action that strengthens you mentally and physically. The key is finding healthy cheat codes that elevate you. Don't use a "cheat code" as an excuse to indulge in unhealthy habits that give you an instant dopamine hit. We're here to become better human beings, not just feel good in the moment.

Once you find a cheat code that works for your season, use it daily until it doesn't work anymore. Some cheat codes work for specific levels or seasons of life. When you level up, you might need to find a new code to match where you're going and keep you moving forward.

Rule #4: No blame, no excuses, just ownership. Blaming shifts control out of your hands and into the hands of someone else. When you take ownership, you take back control. Every decision, action, and outcome is yours to own. When things go sideways, own it, and adjust. When things go right, own that, too, and build on it. Accountability is about facing the hard truths of your decisions and understanding that no matter the difficulties, your life is a reflection of your choices.

Many people waste time blaming their parents, society, or circumstances, but your path is yours to carve. If you're stuck in blame, you'll be stuck in the same place. The game of life requires adaptability, resilience, and taking full ownership of your decisions. The blame game keeps you from progressing while radical ownership pushes you forward.

IMPLEMENTING THE RULES RIGHT NOW

1. **Take inventory of your hand.** What cards were you dealt? Write them down and be honest. Accept them as your reality, then decide how you'll play them.
2. **Identify your cheat code.** Think about which daily habit, routine, or ritual gives you a boost and makes your day better. Be sure that your cheat code is healthy, something that benefits you mentally, physically, or spiritually. If it works, stick with it until it doesn't. Then, find a new one that fits your level.
3. **Cut an excuse today.** Pick one excuse you've been leaning on and let it go. Decide to progress with what you've got, no complaints. You're here to play to win.
4.

PART II: NO BLAME, NO EXCUSES

Blame doesn't change your situation; it just gives you a place to hide from accountability. The more you lean on blame, the more power you give away. Think about that. Every time you point the finger, you're basically saying, "I have no say in my life." You're letting someone else dictate what happens next. If you're serious about winning, you must be real with yourself and cut that nonsense. Blame is a roadblock you willingly put in your own path. Placing blame might feel like a relief at the moment, but it's merely a distraction from getting where you really want to go.

THE POWER OF ACCEPTING THE UNCHANGEABLE

One of the hardest truths you'll face is realizing that some things in life are out of your control.

Your past?

It's done.

Your family?

You didn't pick them.

The starting line you got placed at?

It is what it is.

But here's the twist: Accepting what you can't change doesn't make you weaker. It makes you stronger. When you finally decide to stop wrestling with what's unchangeable, you free up energy to focus on what you *can* change. That's a power-shifter. Most people waste so much time stuck in the past and pointing fingers that they don't see the doors opening right in front of them.

Secure another win by making peace with what's behind you. It's not about forgetting but looking at those experiences and saying, "You made me tougher." Own it, but don't let it own you. Take the lesson and keep it moving. When you're not weighed down by blame, you can fully focus on what lies ahead.

MASTERING THE "OWN IT" MINDSET

Living with zero excuses means taking 100% accountability, but let's be real—taking accountability isn't easy. It's not easy to look at your situation and say, "Yeah, that's on me." But you can't progress if you're still making excuses or blaming everyone else for where you're at. Every setback, struggle, and obstacle you've faced has one thing in common: You. That's not a knock on you but a reminder that you have the power to change the game.

The "own it" mindset isn't motivational fluff; it's a lifestyle. The "own it" mindset means that when something goes sideways, you don't waste time finding someone to pin it on. Instead, you figure out what *you* can do to make it right and do better next time. Success doesn't come from passing the buck; it comes from saying, "This is mine to handle." People who own their lives aren't out here waiting for handouts or sympathy. They're making moves despite obstacles. Every time you choose ownership over excuses, you're building a mindset that says, "I'm in control of this."

INTEGRITY IS THE BACKBONE OF OWNERSHIP

Having integrity means your actions line up with your values, even when no one's watching. When you say you're going to do something, do it. When you commit to a path, follow through. I learned the importance of integrity the hard way. I fell on my face time and time again and missed out on relationships and opportunities because I wasn't living with integrity. There was a potential high-end client who wanted to train with me. At the time, I wasn't fully locked in. I was distracted by people and temptations that didn't matter. This particular client was waiting for me to set them up to begin training, but I totally forgot to put them on the schedule. A week went by, and by the time I realized they had already hit me up, saying, "Never mind, I found someone else. I wanted to start ASAP, and you were taking too long."

This was right after I blew $10K from my savings, money I should've used to build, invest, and set myself up for success. Instead, I wasted it on drinking, excessive partying, and trying to look like something I wasn't. I was caught up in the fast life, making reckless decisions, and chasing validation. In the middle of that chaos, I lost out on a client who could've helped me turn my life around. That moment hit me hard because it wasn't just about losing a client. It was a reflection of my discipline or lack thereof. It was a wake-up call.

That was a turning point for me. I had to get serious. No more half-stepping and no more allowing distractions to keep me from my goals. If you're not fully locked in, life will pass your opportunities to someone who's ready.

Looking back, I realize how my lack of integrity held me back and kept me cycling through the same mistakes. That's why I'm so strong on it now—because I understand what it costs when you don't have it. Integrity isn't just a value; it's a requirement. Integrity is the backbone of ownership. it holds up everything—your character, your reputation, your relationships, and ultimately, your future. Without it, the "own it" mindset falls apart. I learned this by watching opportunities slip away that I could've held onto if I'd just been honest with myself and others. Integrity doesn't just open doors; it keeps them open. And if you're serious about becoming the best version of yourself, integrity is non-negotiable. It will keep you grounded when life gets hard and reminds you to honor your commitments.

WHY INTEGRITY MATTERS TO GOD

God doesn't care about what you accomplish. He cares about how you get there. Integrity isn't just a personal virtue but a reflection of something greater, a reflection of Him. Living with integrity means aligning yourself with values that honor the gifts, opportunities, and responsibilities He's entrusted to you. Every action, word, and commitment reflect the veracity God wants you to develop. When you live with integrity, you're saying, "I value what God has placed in me and honor it fully." It's about respecting the opportunities He's given you and showing that you're trustworthy with them.

God wants you to grow and succeed, but not at the expense of your soul. Integrity is how you keep yourself in check. Integrity will remind you that your actions and words should align with your faith. When you live with that mindset, success becomes meaningful.

IMPLEMENTING THE "NO BLAME, NO EXCUSES" RULE

1. **Reframe your past.** Write down one thing you've blamed others for in the past. Shift your perspective by focusing on what you learned from that experience. How did it make you stronger?
2. **Create a "No Excuse" mindset.** Starting today, catch yourself when you make an excuse. Recognize it, stop it, and shift to an action-oriented mindset. Instead of "I can't because…," ask, "What can I do despite…?"

PART III: OWNERSHIP IN ACTION

It's one thing to talk about accountability, but living it is a whole other story. Ownership in action means showing up with integrity, no shortcuts, and no dodging responsibility. Living this way every day requires consistency and grit. Ownership in action is about making decisions that align with the person you're working to become, not the person looking for the easiest path. The choice to be radically accountable can change the course of your life. It's a mindset that doesn't just stop with words and affirmations; it pushes you to live in a way that demands respect from yourself and others.

LIVING WITH RADICAL ACCOUNTABILITY

Every day, you have the choice to live with accountability or to take the easy route. Set clear intentions, follow through on commitments, and finish what you start. Radical accountability isn't just a philosophy but a practice. If you say you're going to do something, own it completely.

Don't just check boxes for the sake of checking them; handle every commitment knowing it's a direct reflection of your character.

And, yeah, radical accountability can feel uncomfortable, but you must face uncomfortable truths about where you're falling short to actively correct them. The more you practice it, the stronger your accountability muscle becomes. Each decision to show up, be present, and own your actions is a step toward becoming your best self.

DEVELOPING A "NO ESCAPE" MINDSET

When you commit to radical accountability, you cut out the option to escape or find an easy out. There's no room for half-effort or excuses. A "no escape" mindset means you show up or you don't. There's no gray area. I've been in situations where quitting felt easier, and I could've blamed circumstances and walked away, but I stayed because I knew I needed to grow outside of my comfort zone. If I bailed, I would be taking a step back from the person I wanted to be.

When you make a commitment, see it through, even if it means getting knocked down and standing back up again. Every time you choose to stay in the fight, you're building a mindset that won't break at the first sign of hardship. You're developing a mindset that will push you through setbacks and fuel you for long-term growth.

OWNING MY ACTIONS

I take ownership seriously because I view this as a way to honor my father and the principles he stood for. Before my father passed, he tried to instill certain values in me, wisdom I didn't fully appreciate until I got older. One of his most important lessons was about being a man and facing up to my mistakes. He'd always say, "Tell the truth and fix it," drilling into me that real men don't run from what they've done but they face it and make it right. Those words mean everything to me now. My father worked hard to pull himself up from a life of struggle to give me a shot at something better. How dare I disrespect his name by making excuses and not living up to what he taught me?

I mean that.

How dare I disrespect him by not owning up, by using his death as some kind of free pass to dodge life's hard truths?

My father didn't survive a multitude of challenges for me to waste the opportunities his sacrifices made possible. He didn't make it out of that lifestyle for me to just throw it all away. I take my journey personally, so failing at owning my actions would be like throwing dirt on his memory.

My father didn't have an easy path. He dropped out of school after the sixth grade, fell into street life, and had one of the most infamous police chases in Newark history. Basically, he made his share of mistakes. He was a fighter in every sense of the word. He got jumped with metal bats by rivals and ended up in a coma for 48 days. Doctors said he'd never wake up, or if he did, he would be in a vegetative state. But by God's grace, he pulled through, and I believe he made a fully recovery because my grandmother prayed over him every day. And when he came back, he didn't just go back to the life he had. He changed. He gave his life to God and became a father and husband, determined to make sure I didn't end up in the same cycle.

He did everything he could to show me a different path and give me a shot at a better life. I won't bring shame to him by acting like my mistakes or hardships are bigger than the legacy he left behind. He fought to give me a clean slate, and I owe it to him to make the most of it. His life showed me that you can rise above anything if you're willing to face the reality you've created. He paid his dues, and it's my job to keep his legacy alive by living with integrity and holding myself accountable. Every time I own my actions, I honor my father. My life is living proof that his sacrifices weren't for nothing and that his story lives on through me. I'll continue pushing forward, with brutal honesty and without excuses, because that's what he taught me to do. I'm living to make sure his memory is one of strength, redemption, and purpose.

***

I need you to understand me clearly. This isn't about putting myself on a pedestal or trying to make you think I've got it all together. I've been in the trenches, and I know what it's like to fall, feel stuck, and run from yourself, and I'm not just talking about a few missteps here and there. I'm talking about years of hiding from my pain and looking for every possible escape instead of owning up to my life and facing reality.

I tried every route to avoid healing. I used women, bouncing from person to person to numb the pain of heartbreak because I didn't have the strength to face my feelings. I used alcohol and got behind the wheel, which led to a DUI that could've ended my life and someone else's. I turned to lean, thinking it would ease my mind, but it only clouded my thoughts and pulled me further into darkness. And, yeah, I used porn.

Porn became a crutch, an addiction, a way to avoid the emptiness inside of me and to feel something, anything, instead of dealing with what was really going on.

I'm not proud of those truths, but I share this because I know someone out there is going through the same thing, thinking they're alone.

I want you to know you're not.

I took those paths, searching for something to fill the void, and each time, I made the pain worse. Every so-called "escape" was a lie I was feeding myself. I thought I was managing, but I was only digging a deeper hole. None of those choices brought me peace. They didn't make me a better man. If anything, they made me feel weaker, more trapped in my pain.

What finally set me free was facing myself and admitting that I was running from my own life. I'm telling you this because I need you to understand that avoiding your pain won't heal it. You can try every escape you can think of, but reality and truth will catch up with you. At some point, I had to look in the mirror and own my mistakes. All of them. I had to face the reality that the only way forward was through.

So, if you feel like you're too far gone, or that nobody understands, I want you to know I get it. I've been there, and I know life feels unbearable at times, but healing is possible, and facing your pain is the only way out. Owning my actions was a turning point. Taking accountability wasn't easy, and it still isn't, but every time I choose to face my reality, I free myself from the chains I put on my own life.

If I can fight my way out of the darkness, so can you. You have to be sick and tired of being sick and tired. Be real with yourself and decide that enough is enough. Believe that you hold the power to own your life, change, and find healing. And if sharing my struggles can help even one person, then all of this—every painful mistake I've confronted—will have been worth it.

OWNING THE PAIN OF PRETENDING

Let me level with you. There's pain that comes from living a lie, and that pain cuts deep. I'm not talking about pain that fades with time. I'm talking about pain that eats away at you, day after day, because you know you're not being real. I've been a people pleaser, a liar, a thief, and a fake. I put on a persona because I thought that's what would get me through. I thought I had to act a certain way, talk a certain way, and be someone I wasn't to survive. But that survival came at a cost, my dignity, which I wouldn't wish on anyone.

Pretending to be someone you're not brings pain that's impossible to ignore. There were days I'd look at myself in the mirror and try to convince myself that this fake version was who I really was. Deep down, I knew that was a lie. Every time I put on that persona, every time I lied to make people happy or stole to feel like I could keep up, I was betraying myself. I was creating a version of me that I didn't recognize, a version that left me feeling hollow.

That kind of emptiness?

It eats at you.

The persona I put on was this ultimate tough guy—cold-hearted, unbothered, and reckless. I wanted people to think I didn't feel anything, that I was untouchable and immune to pain. Don't get me wrong, I was reckless. I did some crazy things. But I was never the baddest dude in the streets. I wasn't the hardest or the most feared, but I acted like I was because I thought I had to be.

The truth is, I love making people laugh. I love making people feel important. I have a big heart, but I was also trying to survive. I had to go through a lot by myself, and that made me feel abandoned. Instead of admitting that, I pretended like I had life all figured out. I was poor, but I acted like it didn't bother me. I was insecure, but I walked into rooms like I was the most confident person. I was depressed and angry at life, but I acted like pain didn't phase me.

And the thing about bottling that much pain?

It builds.

I was a ticking time bomb, always on edge, ready to explode. And when I exploded, which I often did, it was never at the right time or toward the right people. Most of the time, the people who felt the brunt of my anger didn't deserve it. But that's what happens when you suppress who you really are. You self-destruct.

Living a lie brought unnecessary heartache and regrets that could've been avoided if I'd just been honest with myself. I wanted something more, something real, but I was too caught up in my own web of facades to reach it. Every lie I told to please someone, every time I stole or faked my way through life, I added weight to my heart. I trapped myself in circumstances that didn't align with who I truly wanted to be, and that kind of self-deceit wears you down. It's mentally and emotionally exhausting.

There's also the pain of not feeling peace and the pain of regret. When you're not true to yourself and trying to keep up with a fake image, there is no rest and no room to breathe because you're constantly hustling to keep up and put on a mask that doesn't fit. And then regret seeps in, the crushing regret of knowing that you could've avoided this pain if you had just been real from the start. If you had just owned up to who you are and what you truly want from life instead of bending to others' expectations and approval.

Understand that living in alignment with yourself is non-negotiable if you want to build a life that feels fulfilling, not just one that looks good to others. Pretending, lying, stealing, and putting on a mask—all of it will cost you more than it's worth. None of it is worth the pain, sleepless nights, and sheer emptiness that creeps in when you know you're not being real. You think these tactics are ways to survive, but they're traps that pull you further from the beautiful life God intended for you to live.

If you're struggling with this very battle and caught up in the trap of living a lie, please know you can break free, but breaking free starts with ownership and brutal honesty about the pain you've been creating and carrying. Don't let fear or the need for approval keep you from the peace and freedom that come with living in alignment with who you really are.

THE WEIGHT OF SACRIFICE, SURVIVAL, AND REDEMPTION

Each step forward and every decision to break free from my past has brought guilt. There's a weight that I carry, not just from the sacrifices I've made but from survival. A part of me feels guilty for making it out of circumstances that hold so many people back. I've left people and places behind, and that often haunts me, knowing that while I'm pushing forward, some people never get that chance. That's the weight of survival guilt.

The survival mindset I grew up with shaped me in ways I'm still working to understand. Leaving behind the version of myself that was built to survive and navigate tough environments wasn't easy. It feels like I'm shedding skin, saying goodbye to parts of me that were forged through struggle. you care about are still stuck in cycles you escaped.

Sometimes, I wonder if it's okay to feel good about where I'm headed, knowing others are still fighting similar battles I've already overcome. There's deep-rooted guilt that comes with success and growth when you've made it out. I know what it's like to struggle, and yet here I am, moving forward. Every step I take, I think about those who didn't make it or get the same chances, and this feeling sits heavy on my heart.

Surviving isn't just about moving forward; it's about carrying memories, people, and stories in your heart of where you come from. And that kind of weight doesn't quickly go away. Some nights, survivor's guilt hits hard, making me question if I deserve to be where I am. Thankfully, I'm learning to take this guilt and turn it into fuel. Instead of letting it hold me down, I try to allow it to push me forward. I carry this weight of survival with purpose because if I don't, then everything I've sacrificed and left behind loses its meaning. I owe it to myself—and to those who never got the chance—to make this life count, turning every sacrifice into something meaningful. It's my responsibility to honor this journey and live a life that shows respect for everything I've been through and for everyone who was a part of my story. We can't let the weight of guilt hold us down. Instead, acknowledge this weight as a reminder of where you've come from and of the life you're building now.

I'm not free of this feeling, and I'm not sure I ever will be. But I stay diligent, letting this guilt fuel me, making it part of a story still being written. There's power in survival, taking every sacrifice and struggle and turning it into a life that means more than just getting by.

BREAKING FREE FROM TOXIC BEHAVIORS

Here's something that isn't discussed enough: When you've spent years in survival mode, you pick up behaviors and mindsets designed to protect you in tough environments, but those behaviors can become significant barriers to growth. The process of unlearning, of letting go of habits that once kept you safe but now hold you back, is one of the hardest and most necessary journeys. When you've been taught to survive, thriving doesn't come naturally. Thriving feels foreign, sometimes uncomfortable, because it's unfamiliar.

Survival mode has a way of hardening your spirit. Navigating life in survival mode makes you quick to react, quick to put up walls, and quick to assume the worst because that kept you safe. But that mindset and those defenses keep you from experiencing the life you're trying so hard to build. I had to unlearn behaviors that I had come to accept as part of who I was—the defensiveness, the constant readiness for life to go wrong, and the need to control situations because trusting others felt risky. Over time, I realized that my "survival skills" were holding me back from moving forward.

The process of unlearning is harrowing. You must peel back layers of yourself and strip away parts that are deeply ingrained. Unlearning meant facing the fact that I didn't have to keep my guard up, push people away, or assume that everyone was out to get me. Unlearning meant letting go of quick fixes and the need to stay one step ahead because I was too afraid to face the discomfort of change. At times, I felt like I was losing myself, but I had to remind myself that I wasn't losing anything real; I was merely letting go of what was keeping me stuck.

Unlearning doesn't happen overnight.

Unlearning is a daily process of choosing to respond differently, catch yourself in old habits, and consciously replace them with healthy actions that align with who you're becoming, not who you were.

I had to learn to trust, to let people in, and admit when I didn't have all the answers—because growth requires vulnerability, and survival mode doesn't leave much room for that.

Unlearning is humbling.

There's a certain humility that comes with realizing that the behaviors you once wore, like steel armor, are the very things you must take off to thrive. I used to pride myself on being tough, on being the one who could handle anything. But that toughness prevented me from asking for help, admitting when I was struggling, and letting others see the real me. The unlearning process showed me that true strength isn't in the walls you build but in your willingness to tear them down.

There's freedom on the other side, a freedom to be yourself without the need for constant defense. Unlearning the toxic parts of survival creates space for a healthier, more resilient version of yourself. If you don't let go of survival mode, you'll end up surviving life instead of enjoying it. Thankfully, unlearning creates an opportunity to redefine yourself based on the person you're aiming to become, not on what once held you back.

HOW TO LET GO OF SURVIVAL MODE

Letting go of survival mode isn't a single decision but a daily battle. You don't just wake up one morning and decide you're done with survival mode and suddenly start thriving. It's a process of rewiring your entire mindset, challenging the habits and behaviors that have kept you safe but also kept you stuck. To make this shift, there are several key concepts to understand.

1. Survival mode is not a lifestyle, it's a defense mechanism. Survival mode isn't who you are. It's what you learned to do to make it through tough times. And in many ways, it served a purpose. Survival mode helped you navigate danger, instability, and trauma. It prepared you for the worst. But if you're reading this book, you're probably at a point in life where you're trying to do more than merely survive. You're trying to build something greater for yourself, and that means recognizing that survival mode is no longer serving you, it's stunting you.

The first step in letting go is to acknowledge that you're in survival mode. Ask yourself:

- *Am I always waiting for something to go wrong?*
- *Do I struggle to relax, even when life is going well?*
- *Do I push people away or assume they'll leave?*
- *Am I always on edge or quick to react?*
- *Do I overthink?*

- *Do I avoid being vulnerable because I don't want to get hurt?*

If you answered yes to most of those questions, you're likely operating in survival mode. The good news is that you recognize it and can start unlearning it.

2. Learn to respond, not react. Survival mode makes you react to everything like it's a threat, even when it's not. Someone giving you constructive criticism? You take it as an attack. A friend not responding to your text? You assume they don't care about you. Life throws an obstacle your way? You immediately feel like the universe is against you. Unlearning survival mode means learning to respond instead of reacting. Instead of assuming the worst, pause and take a breath. Ask yourself:

- *Is this a real threat, or am I conditioned to expect one?*
- *Am I responding based on reality or past pain?*
- *What is a healthier way to handle this situation?*

When you start asking yourself these questions before you react, that's when you know you're unlearning survival mode.

3. Trusting the right people and letting go of hyper-independence. One of the biggest lies that survival mode tells you is you can only rely on yourself. That's because, at some point, people may have let you down, abandoned you, or betrayed you. So, you built a wall, thinking, *I got me, I don't need anybody else.* But that mindset will keep you isolated and exhausted.

Unlearning survival mode means allowing yourself to trust gradually. Not everyone deserves your trust, but someone does. Find the people who have shown consistency, pour into you without taking, and show up when you're not at your best. Let them in, even if it's little by little. If you've gone from shutting people out to gradually allowing the right ones in, you're unlearning survival mode.

4. Making decisions from a place of growth, not fear. In survival mode, every decision is about minimizing risk. In survival mode, you don't take chances or step out of your comfort zone. You do what's safe. Unlearning survival mode means shifting from:

- *"I can't take this opportunity because what if I fail?"* to *"If I fail, I'll learn. If I win, I'll grow."*
- *"I can't leave this toxic environment because it's all I know"* to *"I deserve better, and I will build better."*
- *"I need to stick with what's familiar because it's safer"* to *"Familiarity isn't always good. Sometimes it's just comfortable."*

You know you're unlearning survival mode when you stop making choices based on avoiding pain and start making choices based on pursuing growth.

5. Give yourself permission to heal and be happy. This might be the hardest part. After years of just trying to survive, happiness can feel foreign, like you don't deserve it. You might even sabotage your peace because chaos feels more familiar. Unlearning survival mode means giving yourself permission to:

- *Feel joy without guilt*
- *Rest without feeling lazy (I'm still learning this)*
- *Accept love without questioning it*
- *Have peace without waiting for the other shoe to drop.*

If you've ever caught yourself in a good moment and felt like you had to brace for something bad to happen, that's survival mode. When you start allowing yourself to fully enjoy the good without feeling fear, that's when you know you're on a healing path.

FINAL THOUGHTS

Many of us come from environments where struggle was all we knew. And we wear it like a badge of honor, as if enduring hardship makes us stronger, but the truth is, you don't have to stay in struggle mode just because it's familiar. You're allowed to heal. You're allowed to move forward. You're allowed to experience life beyond survival mode. You weren't meant to just make it through life. You're meant to live it. The moment you choose growth over fear, peace over chaos, and love over isolation is the moment you begin to break free. So ask yourself: Are you still surviving or are you finally ready to start living?

CHAPTER TEN: CREATING A ROUTINE THAT ALIGNS WITH YOUR GOALS

PART I: THE ROLE OF ROUTINE IN SUCCESS

Routine might not be what you want to do, but it's what you need. Routine is the price of admission if you're serious about entering the next level of success. Routine isn't fancy nor is routine fun, but routines build consistency, and consistency breeds strength. Often, winning routines include an early-morning alarm. That 4 a.m. wake-up? It's not a motivational gimmick; it's about getting up before the world, putting yourself first, and locking in wins while everyone else is asleep.

Think about that.

While others are dreaming, you're already moving toward yours. That's the edge routine provides.

Once upon a time, every day felt like a mental battle because I was figuring things out as I went. But once I set a routine, life became simpler. My head was clear, and I had the energy to go harder on what really mattered.

Let's be real here. Routines don't just provide structure; they expose your weak points. If you're serious about growth, you'll need to face the areas where you're slacking, and routines will certainly reveal them. Routine doesn't let you hide, so if you're not showing up, your routine will call you out. People may blame time or circumstances; they'll blame anything but themselves. But routines? They demand that you step up. They force you to look in the mirror and see where you're falling short. Because you're either abiding by your routine or you're making excuses and falling short. When I didn't feel motivated, and when life was coming at me from all sides, my routine kept me in the game. Those early mornings weren't glamorous, but they kept me in the fight, and eventually, paid off.

Routines also train you to control your day, not the other way around. When I said routines are like mental armor, I meant it. They shield you from noise, doubts, and outside opinions. When you're locked into a routine, you don't have time for to entertain nonsense. You're too busy making progress to care about what others think or to give in to the voice in your head that says it's okay to slack. Every time you follow through on your routine, you feed your discipline muscle. You're proving to yourself that you're in control and have what it takes to keep going.

If you're out here thinking routines are optional, you're playing yourself. But if you're not willing to put in the work of creating a routine, this book isn't for you. However, if you're ready to step up, stop talking, and start doing, consider this book the blueprint.

Following a routine is also about living with intention. Every action, step, and choice to build the life you want is helping you create something real, not merely go through the motions.

This book?

This is a reflection of the fruits of my routine.

It's proof of what living with intention looks like.

I could've told myself I've already achieved enough, that I'm done healing and evolving. But I set a goal to make this book happen, and every day I showed up to write, sticking to the routine that brought this book from idea to completion.

That's why routines matter.

They're more than a schedule.

They're the blueprint for turning aspirations into action and progress into results.

You want to see progress? You want to look back and know you did everything you could to become the best version of yourself?

Start with your routine.

Set your intention, build your routine, and don't look back.

At the end of the day, routines are about self-respect. Setting a routine and sticking to it is a message to yourself that you are worth the effort, your goals matter, and you're done with excuses. If you're serious about reaching the next level, you need routine. So, set that routine, commit to it, and watch what happens. This isn't about adding structure for the sake of it. This is about becoming unstoppable.

PART II: DESIGNING YOUR IDEAL ROUTINE

Building a routine isn't just about getting things done; it's about setting up a system that aligns with the life you want to create. Building a routine is personal. Your routine needs to fit your goals, schedule, and lifestyle. You're designing something that has to work, day in and day out.

And don't even think about copying someone else's routine.

You have to tailor your routine to your strengths, needs, and goals.

This is about crafting something that positions you for success.

To craft your routine, you need clarity. You can't build a routine if you don't know where you're trying to go. You need a goal, a vision for where you want this routine to take you. Start by asking yourself, "What do I want to achieve?"

Write it down.

Visualize it.

Your routine should be your roadmap to your end goal, not just a checklist of tasks that keep you busy. Without clarity, you'll float through motions without direction.

When I started building my routine, I had to be brutally honest with myself about what I wanted. I knew what I wanted to achieve, and I knew what it would take to get there. There were no shortcuts or magic formulas, just consistent effort. My routine was built around these honest realizations and pure intentions, and I needed to ensure that every part of my routine needed to serve the bigger picture.

Identify key actions that have the greatest impact on your end goal. Don't make the mistake of filling your routine with busy work. It's not about doing more but about doing what moves you closer to your goals. I see people who load up their schedule with a hundred things but never feel closer to their dreams.

Why?

Because they think productivity equates to success. In your routine, focus on what matters. Pick three to five actions each day that directly impact your goal and make those priorities.

The next step? Setting up your routine to win early. I always start my day with something challenging, something that gets me in that winning mindset right away. For me, it's a workout or going for a run. It's about securing that first win before the sun rises, proving to myself that I'm serious about achieving my wildest dreams. When you start your day with something powerful, something that requires effort, it sets the tone for everything else. This earning morning win means you've secured a W before most people open their eyes.

Make your routine adaptable but intentional. Life will throw curveballs, that's a given, but the beauty of a routine is that you have a fallback system. If something doesn't go as planned, you don't just scrap the whole day. You adjust. That's the difference between having a routine and just winging it. A strong routine has room for flexibility. You know your key actions, so if something unexpected arises, you can remain on track by focusing on other essentials within your routine.

For example, I set up my routine around what I can control. My mornings are sacred because that's when I have the most control over my time. Later in the day, life can get chaotic—clients, calls, emergencies. But my morning routine? It's mine. I'm intentional and in control of what happens during those hours. And when life hits, as I know it will, I know I've already locked in my wins. That's the power of designing a routine that serves you, even on hard days.

Start small, then build. Too often, people try to overhaul their entire schedule in one go. They think they need a whole new life overnight, so they set themselves up for failure with unrealistic expectations.

You shouldn't change everything at once.

Start with one habit. A successful routine is about consistency, not intensity. You're aiming to build something sustainable, something you can maintain long after the hype wears off.

Building a routine also forces you to get real about what you're committed to. Anybody can claim they want success, but if your routine isn't backing that up, then you're just talking. Every part of your routine pulls you closer to your goals or keeps you stuck. So, when you're setting up your routine, don't just add tasks. Instead, add actions that make a difference.

Routine teaches you to respect your time. When you don't have a routine, you throw away time on trivial tasks. You waste hours on distractions, scrolling, and procrastinating. But when you have a routine, you're saying, "My time is worth something. My goals are worth something." Cultivating and sustaining a routine shows a different level of respect for yourself and for what you're trying to achieve.

If you're serious about leveling up, you need a routine that's just as serious. Ensure that your routine challenges you and leaves no wiggle room for excuses. Your routine will be the backbone of your transformation. It will push you through hard days, setbacks, and doubts. It's not just about winning the day but setting yourself up for repeated success.

PART III: MAINTAINING FLEXIBILITY WITHIN STRUCTURE

Routine is key, no doubt, but life doesn't care about your plans. Emergencies come up, things go sideways, and some days feel like pure chaos. But here's where people go wrong. They see flexibility as a weakness. They think if they're not hitting every bullet point on their routine, they're failing.

That's not the case.

Power in a routine is knowing how to flex without breaking and how to adapt without losing momentum. The structure of your routine is there to serve you, not box you in.

Think about routine through the lens of an athlete. A boxer doesn't go into the ring with one move. Instead, they're prepared to counter whatever comes their way with an arsenal of moves. That's how you need to treat your routine. Set your tasks but be ready to adjust when life throws punches. But keep in mind that flexibility doesn't mean freedom to go off track. It doesn't mean today's a "free day" because something came up.

Let's say I have a set workout plan in the gym, but I'm traveling or the gym's closed. I don't just skip the workout. I find an alternative like bodyweight exercises, going for a run, or shadowboxing. The workout still happens because that's non-negotiable. Flexibility is about adapting, not abandoning your goals. If you're treating flexibility as an excuse to avoid the work, you're not building resilience. You're building poor habits that will drag you down. When you learn to flow within your structure, you won't be affected by unpredictable circumstances. Instead, you remain in control.

And let's be real, the people who see flexibility as an opportunity to slack are the ones who never move forward. They think it's a pass to sit back, skip steps, and let life just happen to them. Flexibility without discipline is a sure-fire way to waste your potential. If you want to win, flexibility must be paired with focus. You're still intentional, still moving toward the same goals. Don't play yourself thinking you can flex your way out of responsibility. Handle the unexpected with intention.

Let's say a client reschedules with me at the last minute. I don't use that as an excuse to goof off for an hour. Instead, I use that time to study, prepare for another session, or work on content. The work continues. It might look different than planned, but I remain productive. Choose to make your time count, no matter how your day shifts.

Being flexible also keeps you from burning out. When you allow for adjustments, you give yourself the grace to be human. You're not a machine, and some days will demand more from you than you planned. If you're constantly burning yourself out trying to hit every detail and to-do, you'll quit before you see results.

Burnout is real, and I learned that the hard way. There was a stretch when I was training clients back-to-back, creating content, running my business, and barely sleeping. I had this mentality that if I just pushed harder, if I just grinded through the exhaustion, I'd get ahead faster. But instead of making progress, I was breaking down. My body was shot, my mind was foggy, and my motivation, something I thought was unshakable, started slipping away. One morning, I was so drained that I slept through my alarm. I woke up to five missed calls from a client who was already at the gym waiting for me. That had never happened before. I prided myself on always showing up, no matter what, but I had pushed myself past my limits. My body forced me to shut down, and that was my wake-up call to re-evaluate my approach.

I often think of life in this way when it comes to giving your all. Think of it like your phone battery. When your phone is at 80-100% you're excited to use it, running apps, scrolling, taking calls, doing everything without worry. But once your battery hits 20% and you get that low power mode notification, you start being more cautious. And when it drops to 10%, then 5%, panic sets in. You scramble to find a charger before your phone shuts down.

Life is the same way.

You can't give someone 100% if you're operating at 10%. And you're not the only one who suffers—your work, relationships, and the people around you suffer, too. They don't get the best of you because you don't even get the best of you. You can't pour into others when your own battery is drained.

If I kept burning out, I wouldn't be able to show up for my clients, my business, or myself. I had to build a system, a routine, which allowed me to keep going long-term, not just in short, unsustainable bursts. That meant prioritizing recovery, setting a realistic schedule, and understanding that small adjustments didn't mean I was slacking but being wise. Flexibility is a strategy that allows you to keep playing the game instead of getting taken out by exhaustion. Recharge your battery so you can perform at the highest level possible.

Here's the takeaway: Build a routine that's solid but adaptable. Know your non-negotiables, the actions you can't skip. Hold yourself to those. And when life doesn't go as planned, don't lie to yourself and say you've lost momentum. Instead, adjust. Flexibility isn't the enemy of discipline. It's what makes discipline sustainable and keeps you in the game, day after day, no matter what life throws at you.

PART V: CRAFTING A ROUTINE THAT WORKS FOR YOU

An effective routine aligns with where you're headed. Too many people try to adopt routines that sound impressive, but the power of routine is its alignment with your goals and daily realities. If your routine doesn't fit your goals, it won't work for you long-term. The key to building a routine that lasts is making it personal and intentional. It's not about what looks good on paper. It's about what genuinely moves you forward. Here's how to create a routine that works:

Step 1: Remember your why and set your non-negotiables. First things first—know why you're doing this. Your "why" is the driving force. Is it to reach a career milestone? Build mental strength? Improve your physical health? Once you're clear, set a few non-negotiables that support your why. Let's say your goal is to get fit. A non-negotiable might be doing some form of physical exercise every day, even if it's just 20 minutes. Define these so that when life hits, you won't compromise on execution.

Step 2: Design it around your strengths and weaknesses. A routine that aligns with your strengths doesn't mean you avoid hard work. It means you're strategic. If you know you focus better in the morning, set aside that time for your hardest tasks. If you're sluggish mid-afternoon, schedule things like simple follow-ups or tasks that require less intensity. And here's the brutal truth: If you know you struggle with discipline, set up reminders or accountability checkpoints, or enlist a friend to keep you on track. A strong routine accounts for your weaknesses and works with them.

Step 3: Start with small wins to build momentum. One of the quickest ways to build a sustainable routine is to begin with small, doable actions. Maybe it's waking up 15 minutes earlier or taking five minutes to journal at the end of the day. These small wins add up, with each building momentum. Once you see what's possible with a few small wins, you can build bigger, more demanding actions into your day. But remember not to set a huge routine right out of the gate. Start small, build, and keep winning daily.

Step 4: Set a weekly review to adjust and improve. Flexibility with intention will ensure your routine is adaptable for the long haul. Each week, take ten to 15 minutes to review your routine. Ask yourself what's working, what isn't, and what needs to be adjusted. If you notice a certain part of your routine feels forced or unsustainable, don't hesitate to make changes. This isn't about giving up but about optimizing. Your review time is a chance to double down on what's working and cut the distractions.

Step 5: Make time for recovery and reflection. A powerful routine doesn't mean pushing 24/7. It's about being strategic, knowing when to go hard and when to reset. Build time into your week for recovery, whether that's a rest day, time to connect with family, or time to unplug. Without reflection, you'll burn out before you hit your goals. At the end of each day, take a few minutes to check in with yourself: Did you hit your non-negotiables? What could you improve? This is where you adjust your approach, and ensure you're growing, not just going through the motions.

IMPLEMENTING IT TODAY

If you're serious about changing your life, take the above-mentioned steps and put them into action today. Don't wait for the "perfect" time to start because the perfect time doesn't exist. Commit to creating momentum and remember the purpose of your routine: to build, create, and reinforce the habits that support your growth. If you wait, you're only proving to yourself that you're not ready to do what it takes. Start today, adjust as you go, and keep it moving.

CHAPTER ELEVEN: SEPARATING THE COMMITTED FROM THE COMFORTABLE

PART I: WHAT IT MEANS TO HAVE A STRONG WORK ETHIC

Work ethic isn't just about showing up. It encompasses the energy, drive, and mindset you bring to everything you do. My dad drilled that into me from a young age. He wasn't one of those parents handing out "good try" ribbons or participation trophies. In fact, he hated those. I remember coming home with a participation trophy, and he told me, straight up, "We don't keep those in this house. You're the best, and you need to know that."

He made me throw it out.

Harsh? Yeah, but that's where my competitive fire was born. From that moment, I knew I wasn't here to participate. I was here to win.

My dad was my first coach, and he didn't give anything to me for free. We'd go outside to race, and let me tell you, he never "let" me win.

I had to work for it, fight for it, and push myself to the limit. And when I finally beat him for the first time, I felt on top of the world. I still remember that feeling, knowing I earned that victory, and he hadn't slowed down or given me a pass. I outpaced him fair and square, and he was proud because he knew I'd fought for it. Those experiences with my father taught me early on that winning isn't handed over—you have to go out and earn it.

That competitive spirit became part of who I am. In high school, I didn't just get nominated for "Most Competitive" year after year—I won it every single time. The whole school knew how I operated. People would say, "That's Randy Savage, that dude's a dog." Where I come from, when they call you a "dog," it means you're relentless, you're a beast. If we were out there playing pickup basketball or football, I wasn't there to mess around. I was there to win. Losing wasn't an option; it's like my mind couldn't even process it. But I knew that if I wanted to win, I had to grind for it. Nobody was going to hand me anything, and that mindset has been with me ever since.

That hunger to win goes beyond the field or the gym. It's something I carry everywhere, and it started with a simple lesson from my dad: Wins are earned, not given. That's why I don't play around when it comes to my work ethic. I know what it takes because I learned early on that if you want something, you've got to fight for it. The mentality of "no excuses" and "no handouts" shaped me into who I am today.

THE ROLE OF INTEGRITY IN WORK ETHIC

A strong work ethic is impossible to attain and maintain without integrity. There's no such thing as a good work ethic if you're only giving half effort when nobody's watching. Integrity is doing the right thing consistently, even when it's tough or inconvenient. If you're willing to cut corners or compromise your standards to make things easier, then you're not developing a strong work ethic; you're just putting on a show. The real test of your work ethic is staying true to your principles when it would be easier to let them slide.

Integrity in work ethic is about holding yourself to the same standard, regardless of who's watching or what the payoff looks like at the moment. It's about knowing that every time you cheat the process, every time you take the easy way out, you're robbing yourself of growth. That's why integrity is non-negotiable for anyone serious about building an unbreakable work ethic.

KOBE BRYANT: OUTWORKING THE COMPETITION

When it comes to work ethic, nobody embodied it like Kobe Bryant. Kobe wasn't just talented, he was relentless. He had the mindset of not letting anyone outwork him. He was in the gym hours before practice started, shooting, running drills, and sweating it out while everyone else was in bed. Kobe said he put in so much work that by the time others caught up, he was already winding down. That's the kind of mentality that separates the great from the average—the refusal to let anyone outwork you.

Kobe's approach resonates with me because that's exactly how I think about work. When you're out there grinding, it's not just about the hours; it's about the purpose behind every rep. Kobe didn't just go through the motions. He attacked every session like it was game day.

That's the kind of mindset you need if you want to be unbreakable. You're either working to get better or falling behind. Kobe's work ethic serves as a reminder that greatness isn't a random achievement. It's a lifestyle, a commitment to never settling, and a dedication to pushing yourself beyond what you thought was possible.

PART II: STAYING HUNGRY AND AVOIDING COMFORT

Complacency is the enemy of growth. Complacency creeps in after you hit a milestone and think you've "made it." But here's the truth: If you want to build an unbreakable work ethic, you have to stay hungry, keep pushing, and never settle. Comfort is a trap, and the second you start getting comfortable is the second you start slipping. Complacency doesn't look like an immediate fall. Instead, it's slow, subtle, and sneaks up on you when you least expect it. Staying hungry means keeping that fire alive, even after the wins start coming.

FIGHTING THE "GOOD ENOUGH" MENTALITY

One of the quickest ways to get stuck is to believe you've done "enough." The "good enough" mentality is where dreams go to die. I've seen people lose everything because they thought they could coast once they got a little success. They put their guards down, and that hunger to keep pushing faded. But let's be real. Just because you've reached a certain level doesn't mean you're done. That's just the beginning because your goals should change based on your growth. A strong work ethic isn't about reaching a finish line. It's about redefining what "good enough" looks like every day. If yesterday's standards are good enough today, you're not growing; you're just standing still.

I fell into this trap myself. After my first year in Orlando, I felt like I was on top of my game. Business was booming and my name was getting out there, and that's exactly when I let my guard down. I started to relax, thinking I could ease up a bit. I had clients relocating due to new jobs, and instead of hitting the ground to replace them, I told myself I had "done enough."

Big mistake.

Instead of approaching every day like it was war, I got comfortable and paid the price. I forgot that every day is another battle, and if you're not showing up ready to fight, you're setting yourself up to lose. Success doesn't allow for complacency.

That period of my life served as a wake-up call. I realized that "good enough" is an average mentality, and average was never my aim. Getting too comfortable almost derailed my progress. Thankfully, I recognized it early and was able to course-correct. The mentality of "good enough" is dangerous because it sneaks in subtly. You don't realize you're slipping until your results start slipping, too. If you want to avoid this pitfall, remind yourself often that there's always another level, another skill to improve, and another goal to hit. Complacency is like poison, and it only takes a small dose to kill a vision.

That experience taught me that the grind doesn't stop just because you had a good year or reached a new level. The people who last, the ones who keep winning, are the ones who stay hungry. They refuse to let "good enough" enter their vocabulary because they're in constant pursuit of greatness and never settle for yesterday's wins.

CULTIVATING A BEGINNER'S MINDSET

One of the best ways to keep complacency in check is to approach each day like a beginner. When you're starting out, you're hungry to learn, willing to put in the hours, and open to new ways to grow. But as you progress, that openness may fade. You start thinking you know it all, and the downhill slide begins. A beginner's mindset keeps you sharp, humble, and, most importantly, hungry.

This pride of thinking you "know it all" is a dangerous lie. Nobody knows it all, and the second you start believing you do, you're setting yourself up for failure.

I know this to be true because I've been there.

After a certain level of success, I thought I had all the answers, and that pride almost cost me everything. I stopped asking questions, stopped seeking feedback, and started believing my way was the only way. That mindset didn't just hurt my business, but it held me back from growth in my personal life. Pride might give you a temporary high, but it'll take you down just as fast if you're not careful.

Humility is the antidote to pride. God honors humility. When you remain open, vulnerable, and willing to show your flaws, you not only help others, but you create space for blessings to flow into your life. When you carry humility, you allow yourself to be teachable. The humility to know you don't have it all figured out is what God uses to protect and cover you. Humility keeps the door open for God to do His work, correct you, and cover you when pride would have left you exposed. Embracing that humility keeps you grounded and ensures complacency does not sneak in.

Those who thrive treat every day as an opportunity to improve, absorb something new, and refine their skills. A beginner's mindset is one of the most powerful weapons you can have in your arsenal. It keeps you grounded, open, and from getting blindsided by pride. Remember: If you're not growing, you're moving backward.

Having that mindset is about more than avoiding complacency. It's about resilience. It's about bouncing back from failures, learning from every setback, and using those lessons to fuel your next move. A true beginner's mindset makes you adaptable, ready to pivot, and prepared to face any challenge. It's a mentality that ensures readiness for the next step, next level, and next lesson.

THE FEAR OF GROWTH AND COMFORT'S TRAP

Fear of growth is real, and it's often masked by comfort. People say they're comfortable where they are, but in reality, it's often a cover for fear of change, fear of failure, or fear of what's next. Growth requires stepping into the unknown, and that can be intimidating. Comfort, on the other hand, feels safe. Comfort is predictable, routine, and easy. But the price of staying comfortable is much higher than the price of pushing yourself to grow.

Fear of growth shows up in subtle ways, often disguised as "contentment" or "stability." But deep down, there's a nagging feeling that you're meant for more, that there's a next level calling you, even if you're not sure what that looks like. And the uncomfortable truth is that fear won't go away until you face it. When you cling to comfort because you're afraid of what's next, you're denying yourself the opportunity to discover what you're truly capable of.

I know this firsthand.

There have been times in my life when I stayed in one place too long, not because it was the right place but because it was safe. I let fear of what might happen hold me back, convincing myself I didn't need to change or risk anything. But each time I stayed in that place of comfort, I also felt stuck, as if I were slowly suffocating my own potential. Fear thrives in comfort zones because comfort gives you a reason not to confront it.

Stepping out of comfort doesn't mean diving into chaos but acknowledging the growth that comes with uncertainty and choosing to pursue it anyway. Fear will always be there, but courage moves you forward in spite of it. When you step out of comfort, you make a choice to believe in something bigger and trust that you're capable of handling what's next, even if you don't see the whole path yet.

Comfort zones are just that—zones. They have limits and walls, and they will always hold you back from the potential on the other side. Growth requires you to break through those walls, leave behind the familiar, and step into the unknown. This type of bold leap requires faith, courage, and a belief in yourself that's bigger than any excuse comfort provides. Allow your fear to fuel you. Push past it and watch how your life transforms.

To build an unbreakable work ethic, you must operate as the best version of yourself, but you can't do that if you're carrying a broken soul. Healing is not just a self-care phrase but a requirement for a healthy life. You can work hard, achieve success, and put up a strong front, but if you haven't faced what's broken inside, you'll always be working with a limit on your potential. The best version of you, the one capable of sustained effort, comes through healing. And here's the hard truth: Healing isn't comfortable. Healing hurts. Healing is one of the scariest, most challenging journeys you can take because it requires you to dig up parts of yourself that you may have buried because they were too painful to face. Healing demands that you stop ignoring your scars, traumas, and wounds that hold you back. Healing makes you confront the weight that hasn't been lifted from your spirit, even if you're afraid of what you'll find. But the person you become on the other side of that healing is where peace and transformation lie.

I'm tearing up as I write this because healing began when I started pursuing a relationship with God. I was broken, hurting, and stuck in patterns that kept me in my brokenness. I endured trauma and hurt from others and inflicted pain on myself through poor choices. But in that brokenness, I realized I needed something bigger than myself because working hard without healing only got me so far. My pursuit of God began a deeper transformation, the kind of transformation that lasts, grounds you, and builds you into a person capable of more than you thought possible.

Healing isn't just about dealing with the pain of the past but breaking free of the chains that keep you from becoming who you're meant to be. When you start to heal, you release the burdens that hold you down and block you from growth. Healing brings freedom, and freedom brings clarity. And with that newfound clarity, your work ethic takes on an elevated level of power because you're no longer battling inner turmoil every day. Healing removes inner obstacles that drain you, leaving you with revitalized energy, strength, and resilience that you didn't have before.

To become the best version of yourself, you have to face the hard, uncomfortable work of healing. You must confront the things you'd rather leave in the dark and let God walk you through them. This is a journey, not a one-time fix, and it will stretch you in ways you never expected. But through the stretching and discomfort, you will be rebuilt into someone stronger, wiser, and more resilient.

If you're serious about being the best at what you do, you can't skip the healing process. Trauma, heartbreak, and regret will weigh on you and shape how you show up every day. Unhealed pain creates yet another wall between you and your potential. But when you start to heal, those walls come down, and that's when you can truly give your all, commit to your work, and dive into what you're capable of achieving. Healing doesn't make you perfect; it makes you whole. And when you're whole, that's when the best version of you can finally emerge, fully equipped to live a life of purpose.

A PATH TO STRENGTH AND PEACE

Healing is one of the hardest battles you'll ever face, but it's also one of the most rewarding. Healing doesn't happen overnight. It's an ongoing journey. I'm still learning, growing, and yes, still healing, but

I know each step I take toward healing makes me stronger, gives me more peace, and allows me to help others in ways I once couldn't. The best version of me comes from the scars that I've learned to embrace, not hide from. And the best version of you will arise when you face your scars.

There's this saying many of us have heard time and time again: "God gives His hardest battles to His strongest soldiers." We throw it around, and sometimes, it feels like just another phrase. But when life hits you, and it feels like the weight of the world is crashing down, that's when you start to realize the truth behind it. I know it may feel like you're carrying the heaviest load, like you're the one taking on the hardest battles. But let me tell you something. It's an honor that God trusts you as much as He does. He sees you as one of His strongest warriors, handpicked to take on what most wouldn't survive. You're not just anyone to Him. You're chosen.

Think about it. In ancient days, kings didn't send just anyone to fight battles. They appointed their strongest warriors, those who had proven themselves in the field, could take on the beast, and come out victorious. That's how God sees you. He gives you these battles not to break you, but to build you, refine you, and prepare you for something greater. Every pain and hardship is molding you into a warrior, someone who can face life's storms and prevail.

I used to cry out, "I don't want to be the strongest soldier!" The pain felt like too much, and I was tired of feeling broken, tired of the constant battles, and tired of life itself. As a child who was ready to end my pain for good, I thought if I just bled out, I'd finally have peace. But anytime

I thought I couldn't push through the pain, I somehow made it to the other side. Each time, I emerged a little stronger and a little wiser.

And just to let you know, I am no more special than you. I am no different than you. I don't have a supernatural ability to endure more pain than anyone else. I don't have exclusive resilience that's only reserved for a select few. So if I made it out, so can you. If I survived, you can, too. The only difference between those who make it through and those who don't is the decision to keep going when it hurts, when it's ugly, and when you don't see the light yet.

I didn't do this alone, and it certainly wasn't just sheer willpower that got me through. With God, we can do all things. Not some things, but all things. We are overcomers, built for more than suffering.

You may feel like you're drowning but understand that you have the strength to make it through. If you're still here, and still breathing, that means your story isn't over. There is more for you, but you must be willing to fight for it. Don't count yourself out because God already counted you in.

And so I'm encouraging you to start your healing journey, not for anyone else, but for yourself. Healing does not mean you'll be free from struggle, but it does mean that you'll be free from the pain that's been holding you back. The weight will lift, little by little, and you will find the strength you didn't know you had. Healing won't erase your scars, but you will be able to wear them with pride, as each scar becomes a part of your story that only you can tell, a story that has the power to inspire others.

Every battle you face has a purpose. It might not make sense in the middle of it but trust that each battle is preparing you for something greater. When you choose to heal, you're choosing to step into the person you were meant to be. Healing brings peace, but more than that, it brings a sense of purpose, knowing that everything you've been through wasn't for nothing. God didn't put you through this to watch you suffer. He put you through the battle to build you up, refine you, and make you into the warrior you're meant to be, so take that first step, even if it's small. Allow yourself to face the pain to let go of the weight you've been carrying for too long.

You are not alone.

You have strength inside that's been there all along, just waiting for you to tap into it.

Give yourself a chance to meet that version of yourself. Don't hold back because of fear, shame, or what has happened in the past.

Choose healing.

Choose growth.

Choose to become the best version of yourself, not for anyone else, but for you.

There will be days when you want to quit, days when the pain feels too raw and the scars too deep. In those moments, it's okay to break down and feel every bit of that pain, but don't let your feelings keep you stuck. Feel it, and then let it push you forward.

Each step in healing is like peeling back layers of armor you didn't realize you were wearing, multiple layers that once protected you but now hold you back. Healing asks you to let go of those defenses, confront the pain directly, and trust that you can make it through. While you may feel as though you're tearing down everything you thought you knew about yourself, it's through your vulnerability that you can build a life that's truly yours.

And here's another beautiful aspect of the journey: When you heal, you make room for peace. The peace that comes on your healing journey is more than a feeling of relief; it is part of a solid, healthy foundation. This level of peace is something that no one can take from you because you fought for it, sacrificed for it, and earned it. And that peace stays with you, even when life throws more punches. Healing doesn't mean you won't face any more battles, but it does mean that you'll face them as a whole person who knows they can face whatever comes next.

Healing also gives you a new perspective. It teaches you gratitude amid pain. You start to see how every battle shaped you and every setback taught you something you couldn't have learned any other way. You start to appreciate the strength it took to survive and the courage it took to keep going. And once you've tasted that freedom, there's no going back because you wholeheartedly accept that every moment of discomfort was worth the growth. That's why I'm urging you to take this step. It might feel like climbing a steep mountain, but with every bit of progress, you'll realize how far you've come and how much lighter your heart and mind feel. One day, you'll look back and see that the climb was never about the struggle but about becoming the person you were always meant to be.

Don't wait for the "right" moment to begin your healing journey. The right moment is actually right now. Choose to heal, face what's holding you back, and finally let go of the weight that's been dragging you down. You deserve to know what it feels like to live without the chains of past hurt. You deserve to feel whole, strong, and worthy of a life that's more than survival. You're stronger than you think, and you're capable of more than you know. Step into the journey and give yourself permission to heal.

A LETTER TO THE YOUNGER ME

Dear Younger Me,

I know you're struggling. I know the weight you're carrying feels unbearable at times. The tears, the anger, the fists clenched in pain, the nights spent staring at the ceiling, wondering why life seems so hard, it all feels like too much. But I need you to know something. Every tear, every ounce of pain, and every battle builds you up for something bigger. Those tears you're shedding? They're filling up the bucket that will one day overflow with blessings. You can't see it now, but this pain is laying the foundation for the bright future you're destined to have.

Those fists of anger and battles you're fighting alone in the dark? They're shaping you. They're building a strength within that most people will never understand. One day, when you look back, you'll see that these were the moments that turned you into a warrior with a purpose. You'll realize that the nights you thought would break you actually built you. Every hardship you're facing is preparing you to handle the blessings and responsibilities that are coming your way.

Thank you for not giving up. Thank you for pushing through when it would've been easier to quit. Thank you for staying humble and allowing yourself to be molded instead of becoming hardened by what you endured. Thank you for the risks you took, the leaps of faith, and the moments you chose growth over comfort. Those choices are why I'm standing tall today. You didn't know it then, but you were creating a legacy, one that would impact your life and the lives of everyone you would touch.

Keep fighting and keep believing. You are more than your pain and mistakes. The battles you're facing will one day be the victories you tell others about. One day, you'll be able to look back and say, "I made it through, and it was worth every tear."

With all the love and gratitude,
Future You

A PRAYER OF STRENGTH AND COURAGE

Before I get into this prayer, let me be real with you. I'm a man from the streets. I've made my share of mistakes, committed crimes, and lived a life that most people would judge. I left the church for over ten years because I couldn't stand the fake people or judgments. I'm not here to judge or to preach, and this isn't about pushing religion or telling you what you have to believe. This is just me, sharing truths from my heart. Take these prayers as words of encouragement or utilize this as a moment to recharge. The following prayer was created to lift you up, remind you of your strength, and help you find the courage to keep going, even when life feels like it's building a wall of steel blocking you from everything you deserve

Dear God,

I come to You for strength, not just for me but for anyone reading these words and needing the courage to keep going. I pray that they feel Your presence in their life and that they find the power to push forward, even when the weight feels too heavy. Remind them that every tear, hardship, and struggle is not wasted but a part of a greater purpose and plan that they might not understand but will one day make perfect sense.

Lord, I ask that You show them what's on the other side of their pain. Show them that their battles are shaping them and that their struggles are building strength that will one day be a blessing to themselves and others. Fill them with hope when they feel hopeless, strength when they feel weak, and a reminder that You're walking this journey with them every step of the way.

God, I ask that You help them find peace amid chaos. Please grant them the courage to face all obstacles in their path. Let them know they are not alone and that You've given them everything they need to make it through. May they see that they are strong, loved, and destined for greatness.

In Jesus' name, Amen.

HOW TO IMPLEMENT THIS CHAPTER IN YOUR LIFE

While our prayers certainly hold power, faith without works is dead (James 2:26). In other words, change also comes from action. Here's how you can put this chapter to practice in your life:

1. **Acknowledge your pain and start your healing journey.** Reflect on areas in your life that feel unresolved or hurtful. Acknowledge these feelings instead of suppressing them. Consider journaling, talking with a friend or mentor, or seeking professional support. Healing is a process, so be patient with yourself, and know that progress is still progress, no matter how small.
2. **Set small goals.** Healing and growth don't happen overnight. Set small, daily goals that contribute to your mental, emotional, and physical well-being. Perhaps you take part in ten minutes of quiet reflection each morning, commit to moving your body daily, or take time to do something you love each week. Focus on small steps, knowing they're adding up to big changes.
3. **Create a daily reminder of your strength**. Write down something that motivates you—a quote, a goal, or a memory of overcoming a past struggle—and place this somewhere you'll see daily. Let this

serve as a reminder that you've faced hard times but have the strength to keep going.

4. **Accept imperfection**. Healing isn't about becoming perfect. It's about becoming whole. Accept that mistakes and setbacks are parts of the journey, and don't beat yourself up over them. Embrace your progress, even if it doesn't look like someone else's. You're on your own path, and that path is valuable.

5. **Celebrate small wins.** Each step toward healing is a victory. Don't wait until you're "fully healed" to celebrate yourself. Acknowledge every small win and every moment of growth. Allow yourself to feel proud of how far you've come, no matter how much further you have to go.

6. **Find your support system**. Healing doesn't have to happen in isolation. Surround yourself with people who lift you up, encourage you, and remind you of your worth. These are the people who will be there on tough days and will remind you of your strength when you can't feel it.

7. **Trust the process and stay connected to your "why."** Remember why you started this journey. Trust that each step is part of a greater plan. Hold on to your "why," the reason you want to heal, grow, and become the best version of yourself. Let your "why" be your anchor, the driving force that keeps you going.

CHAPTER TWELVE: SURROUNDING YOURSELF WITH THE RIGHT PEOPLE

THE POWER OF YOUR CIRCLE

Your circle can make or break you, especially when it comes to reaching your goals. Think about this: Everyone in your life influences you, either pushing you closer to who you want to become or pulling you away from it. We hear this all the time, but it's true—you're the average of the five people you spend the most time with. So, surround yourself with people who grind, who hold you accountable, and who challenge you, and you'll start to see that energy flow into your life. If the people around you are making excuses, full of, or playing it small, their energy will seep into your life.

The importance of one's circle became real to me in college, namely with the people I chose to keep close. Me and my friends, Bryce Council, KJ Speller, and PJ Saracino shared a bond that was built not just on friendship but on a shared mission to defy the odds. Each of us came from different backgrounds, but we had something in common: Success wasn't handed to us. Instead, we made a commitment to cultivate it ourselves. Bryce was the one who came to us with the idea for Count Yourself In (CYI), and he asked if we'd stand with him to make something out of nothing. My answer was simple: "I'm in," and that's how CYI was born. We later turned this into a clothing brand, "CYISOON," standing for "Count Yourself In and Make Something Out Of Nothing." Each of us brought authenticity to the table, and together, we made something bigger than our circumstances, upbringing, and battles. Bryce dealt with being undersized and overlooked on the court while facing family challenges that made him question his path. KJ faced his own obstacles, navigating the reality of being adopted and the layers of identity that came with it. PJ was in and out of the game, battling injuries year after year that threatened his athletic career. And me? I came from a background that didn't promise success, just struggle.

We worked countless hours, filming commercials, designing clothes, and selling to peers. Our dorm room became the place where dreams were nurtured. We weren't just building a brand. We were building a movement that shared this underlying message: "You may not have it all now, but if you count yourself in, you can make something out of nothing." Our vision wasn't based on the cards we were dealt but on our determination to play them with everything we had. Having a circle like that transformed my life. We didn't just talk big, but we followed through, together, and that made all the difference.

IDENTIFYING POSITIVE VS. TOXIC INFLUENCES

Not everyone around you is meant to be in your corner. Some people show up as friends, but their energy pulls you down or distracts you from your goals. Toxic influences aren't always obvious. Sometimes, it's the friend who doubts everything you say, or the one who's always gossiping or complaining. These relationships drain you, not fuel you.

Evaluating relationships requires honesty.

Who brings out the best in you?

Who challenges you to think bigger, act better, and stay disciplined?

On the flip side, who drains you?

Who do you feel worst around?

Who makes you feel as though you need to justify your goals?

Recognizing these influences is crucial for protecting and nurturing your growth.

Over time, I've had to let go of certain people, even those I grew up with. It wasn't a matter of judging them but protecting my energy. One of the hardest lessons I had to learn was letting go of someone I used to party with often. When I reached a season where I needed to fully lock in and make sacrifices, I thought he'd understand. I figured he'd encourage me and respect that I was grinding for something bigger. Instead, he was offended. He felt like I was "changing on him." The truth is, I was changing. I was growing, maturing, and locking in for my future. But I wasn't changing on him. I was evolving for me. I could party after I had handled my business, but because he didn't see it that way, he started talking badly about me.

That's when I realized that not everyone will understand your growth. It's not that they were never for you; it's that they haven't reached a similar level of understanding. They haven't experienced what it's like to sacrifice short-term fun for long-term success, so they can't comprehend why you're making those choices.

And that's okay.

Some people need more time, and some may never get there, but that shouldn't stop you from doing what you need to do. You can't wait for everyone to catch up while you're already running toward your purpose.

Growth requires boundaries. If someone around you is comfortable remaining the same, they're likely to pull you down when you start to rise. That doesn't mean you have to cut people off, but it does mean you must recognize who supports your journey and who's merely along for the ride. I had to learn this the hard way, but it one's energy isn't pushing you forward, you're better off without it.

BUILDING A SUPPORTIVE TRIBE

Building a circle that pushes you, inspires you, and holds you accountable doesn't happen by accident. You have to be willing to put yourself out there, connect with people who share your values, and even seek those who are a few steps ahead. These are the people who see potential in you before you see it in yourself.

The bond I formed with Bryce, KJ, and PJ wasn't just about friendship but about holding each other to a high standard. When I'd feel like slacking off, Bryce would remind me why we were grinding in the first place. When PJ struggled with injuries, we'd lift him up and encourage him to keep going. We made a pact to call each other out on any excuses because we knew that each of us had too much at stake to play it small. That mentality carried me through college and well into my career, reminding me that a strong circle will always push you to your potential.

If you're struggling to find a supportive tribe, start by putting yourself in environments where growth is the norm. Attend networking events or find groups online where people are working toward similar goals. Remember that friendship is a two-way street, so show up for others with the same energy you expect people to share with you. When you support and encourage others, you attract people who are willing to do the same for you.

THE POWER OF BROTHERHOOD AND ACCOUNTABILITY

There's something incredibly powerful about brotherhood and having people in your life who keep you grounded and focused. My circle became my anchor and a place where I could admit my fears, be vulnerable, and still be respected. We celebrate each other's wins, push each other through the losses, and set standards for each other that keep us from slipping back into old habits. I'm grateful for these bonds because I wouldn't be here without them. While each person in my tribe took separate paths after college, grinding hard and making moves, we somehow ended up in the same state. As grown men, we're still there for each other, pushing one another to new heights, working out together, and motivating each other daily. From those college dorm rooms to where we are now, we've seen each other grow, struggle, and succeed. Every time we push each other to level up, we're reminded that a strong circle is more than just a college phase but a lifelong connection that keeps us accountable to our goals.

Your tribe is out there, but it's up to you to seek our quality people and to be the kind of person they'd want in their circle. Show up ready to grow, bring positive energy, and be someone others can rely on. When you become that kind of person, you attract people who operate on that same level.

BUILDING A CIRCLE THAT ELEVATES YOU

A powerful circle isn't just about who's beside you in the daily grind but about the people who open doors, speak your name in rooms you haven't stepped into, and protect your reputation when you're not around. The right people recognize your work, see your value, and advocate for you in ways that push you forward.

But this goes both ways.

When your people are out there putting their names on the line for you, speaking highly of you, and setting you up with new opportunities, the last thing you should do is show up halfway. Providing mediocre work, or anything less than your best, isn't just letting yourself down but it's disrespectful to those who vouch for you. Every time I step up to train a client, speak on a stage, or take on a new project, I carry the credibility that my friends and supporters have lent me. They've helped elevate my career by using their networks, sending clients my way, and connecting me with stages to speak on, and brands to collaborate with. When I seize these opportunities, I know my work reflects on them, too.

So, how dare I not show up as my best self when they've gone to bat for me?

That's how you show true respect and love to your friends—by honoring their belief in you through your actions. When you deliver at your highest level, their word gains strength, their voice has more credibility, and your circle grows tighter. It's a cycle. When they speak highly of me, I have to be that person they believe in, and when I live up to it, I protect their word, their reputation, and my word and reputation as well.

Are you showing up in a way that honors the people who believe in you? Do you demonstrate integrity in every move, respect the voices that lift you up, and show up as someone they can stand behind with pride. Because when you do that, you're not just proving yourself but you're proving them right. That's how you give back to the people who invest in you, by showing up as your best self.

STEPS TO BUILD AND STRENGTHEN YOUR CIRCLE

1. **Define what you need**. Be specific about what you value in others. For example, integrity, ambition, and loyalty. Be specific about what you're unwilling to tolerate.

2. **Evaluate your current circle**. Take a hard look at the people closest to you. Are they helping you grow or holding you back? Make the tough calls where you need to.

3. **Put yourself in growth-oriented spaces.** Spend time where growth is valued. Attend events, join groups, and seek places where people with similar values hang out.
4. **Be willing to give as much as you get**. Building a strong circle is a mutual effort. Support others, offer encouragement, and show up for people the way you want them to show up for you.
5. **Be open to change.** Embrace people who come and go. Sometimes, growth means growing apart, and that's a part of the journey, too.

IDENTIFYING POSITIVE VS. TOXIC INFLUENCES

Not everyone who smiles at you is actually for you. Some people wear masks. They might seem supportive, but their actions, words, or energy tell a different story. Learning how to pick out who's truly in your corner versus who's just taking up space is essential for nurturing your growth and staying locked in on your goals.

Toxic influences don't always come with warning signs. A toxic influence could be that friend who always doubts you or throws subtle jabs at your dreams disguised as "advice." They're the ones who stay silent when you win or find ways to downplay your achievements. And let's not forget about the people who act supportive to your face but are quick to talk behind your back when you're not in the room. These types of people are deadly to your growth. Respect your journey enough to only keep people around who genuinely have your back.

I had to learn this the hard way. I used to think loyalty meant sticking by the people I grew up with, no matter what, even if their energy was draining me. But I realized that loyalty isn't about keeping people in your circle who make excuses, doubt your grind, or throw shade when you're making moves. Loyalty is about surrounding yourself with people who want to see you win, push you forward, and check you when you're off your game. I had to make tough calls, cut some ties, and distance myself from those who couldn't align with my mindset. Severing these ties hurt but letting go allowed me to release the weight that was holding me down, which helped me move with stronger momentum. My vision became clearer, and so did my path.

If you're serious about leveling up, ask yourself the following questions:

Who challenges me to grow?

Who claps when I win and doesn't secretly hope for my downfall?

On the flip side, who do I make excuses for, defend, or feel drained around?

This isn't about pointing fingers. It's about being honest with yourself and choosing the people who add fuel to your fire, not oil. The people who truly care will check in on you, tell you uncomfortable truths, and push you forward without tearing you down.

When you sever certain ties, your circle will shrink, and that's fine. Quality over quantity. I'd rather have a tight group of three people who believe in me, support me, and keep me accountable than a crowd of so-called friends who don't care if I succeed or fail. Protect your energy, value your future, and choose people who want to see you win as badly as you do.

SHOUTOUT TO MY BOYS FROM JERSEY

Allow me a moment to highlight some of the most important people who've played a major role in my journey. These are my boys from

Jersey, my squad from high school, who I still call my dawgs and my brothers. (And who would have thought crazy ol' Savage, once a wild kid, is now an author of a self-help book? Surreal.) This shoutout is for Simpkins, Jonathan, Reek, Mali, Whitty, Scheme, Zyair, Dave, David Garcia, Tyron, AK, my cousin Kort, Zhamir, and my cousin Dandre Hull (rest in peace, Dandre). These men have supported me no matter how far I've moved and through every transition, from being the street dude with an edge to becoming a motivational speaker and trainer.

To see us all now, evolving from "bad kids" who were doubted and overlooked to successful Black men, is nothing short of an honor. Life hasn't been easy, and we didn't make it this far by playing it safe. Thank you, my brothers, for sticking by me and holding me down during the toughest times. Thank you for not judging me when I made mistakes and for being the first to help me up when I fell. Thank you for being down to fight with me when things got rough and for checking me when I needed a reality check. Thank you for being who you are, solid and real. As I grow and continue on this journey, I pray you all keep growing with me. One day, I hope we sit around as granddads and granduncles, telling these stories to our future generations, showing them that no matter where you start, where you end up is a choice you make every day.

RECOGNIZING YOUR SUPPORT SYSTEM

For anyone reading this, take a moment to reflect on the people who have been there for you. Reach out to them, thank them, and show them gratitude for holding you up when you were falling. In today's world, it's easy to claim that you did it all by yourself. Social media has made that look like the ultimate badge of honor but let me keep it real with you. Saying you got here on your own is an unhealed, prideful statement. Humans thrive off of support and connection. God did not intend or design life to be lived alone.

Think about it. At some point on your journey, someone extended a hand, offered a kind word, opened a door, or created an opportunity when you thought there was no way out. God's grace and the help of other humans move us forward. No matter how strong, independent, or capable you are, nobody makes it alone. Whether it was your boys hyping you up, a mentor providing guidance, or a stranger who showed you kindness at the perfect time, people make a difference.

Show gratitude to the positive people in your life. It doesn't matter if they're close or distant, whether they extended small acts of kindness or grand gestures. Acknowledge their role in your growth. Send that text, make that call, or meet them in person and give thanks. It's not just about saying the words but truly recognizing that while your grind and resilience have been critical to your success, it's the people who believed in you and stood by you that helped you push through. Gratitude is a mark of growth, a reminder that while you've worked hard, you've also been blessed with people who've had your back.

BUILDING BUSINESS RELATIONSHIPS

When people talk about building relationships, it's easy to think of close friends and tight-knit circles. But if you want to elevate in life, you need to understand that business relationships hold significant weight, too. Everyone in your life doesn't need to be your best friend, but professional connections should still be nurtured and respected. The right network can open doors you didn't know existed.

I've been blessed to have friends and solid acquaintances, people I've done business with, collaborated with, and positioned myself to work with in the future. I'm a high-energy guy, and I bring that energy with me wherever I go. When people see me, I aim to make them smile, share my vibe, and build a positive atmosphere.

Why?

Because positivity and respect go a long way, not just for the sake of being a decent human but also for one's career.

Your reputation, your "face card," should always be valid. This is what people remember when you're not in the room. You might run into someone at an event, a private dinner, or in passing. If you're known for being authentic, you're more likely to get a nod of acknowledgment that can lead to big opportunities. Maybe you've struggled to secure a contract, but then you run into someone you've always been kind to, and suddenly, they pull strings for you. That type of relationship-building can make or break you in the business world.

Here's an example. One of my most notable clients, a high-profile celebrity, came to me through the connection I described above. It started with their manager, who happened to be a mutual friend I met long before I knew they were tied to anyone famous. We shared good energy and had positive interactions, building a small yet meaningful connection. Months later, that manager introduced me to the celebrity, and just like that, I had a new client. My consistent nature and energy had built a certain level of trust that reaped this outcome. That's the power of treating people well without expecting anything in return.

These types of relationships are just as important as close friendships. You never know who knows who, and you never know when you'll need to build your network. Whether someone is speaking highly of you in a meeting or offering you a chance to collaborate, acquaintances can be game-changers.

So, how do you build business-like connections?

Simple.

Consistently show up as your best self.

It's not about being fake or putting on a show but genuinely and consistently showing up with good energy.

It's crucial to remember that being reliable and high-energy isn't for the sake of getting something in return. It's about understanding that each encounter matters. Maybe you don't land a new deal today, but the impression you leave could bring unexpected opportunities down the line. So don't overlook the value of building professional connections. Treat others with respect and dignity. Be that person who brightens someone's day, shows up with a can-do attitude, and makes people feel seen and valued. When the time comes, those moments of shared energy and kindness can lead to your next big break.

KEEPING YOUR FACE CARD STRONG

One of the biggest lessons I've learned is that consistency in how you present yourself builds a reputation that speaks louder than words. In business, your face card, your reputation, becomes your most valuable asset. You could be the most skilled person in the room, but if your energy is inconsistent or if people never know which version of you they're going to get, you become a liability. People gravitate toward those who make them feel good and show up with a genuine, uplifting spirit every time.

I can't tell you how many opportunities have come my way, not because I was the best in the field but because I was known for being reliable. Even when life throws challenges my way, I make sure that doesn't affect the energy I bring to the room. People remember more than you may realize. Whether it's a firm handshake at an event or a friendly, quick conversation in passing, those moments stick. And when the time comes for someone to decide who they want on their team or who they're willing to vouch for, guess whose name they'll bring up? Yours, if you've been consistent.

Cultivating these connections is also about authenticity. There's a difference between being nice because you want something versus genuinely showing up with a good heart. People are discerning. I've seen people try to fake their way through connections, only to be exposed, but when you're real and consistent from the start, people begin to trust you, and trust in business is everything.

Being the person who lifts others up, shares good energy, and who isn't just looking out for themselves creates a ripple effect. You'll find that people will go out of their way to do the same for you. You might be in a tough spot one day, struggling to make a move or unsure how to break through to the next level. Well, because you've been consistent and authentic, you've planted seeds that will sprout. Maybe someone you barely remember from a past networking event hits you up with an opportunity or a lead, simply because you left a lasting, positive impression.

BUILDING BRIDGES WITHOUT BURNING THEM

Another aspect of nurturing business relationships is knowing how to maintain them without burning bridges. Not every relationship will turn into a lifelong bond, and that's okay. Sometimes business paths diverge, and people move in different directions, but how you handle those shifts matters. Parting ways doesn't have to mean cutting ties with resentment. Maintaining respect, even when you no longer work closely together, keeps that door cracked open for the future.

I've been in situations where things didn't work out as planned, and while it was easy to feel frustrated or want to walk away with a chip on my shoulder, I chose to remain respectful. Fast forward months and years later, those same people have reached out with new opportunities or have spoken positively about me in rooms I wasn't in. You never know where life will lead you or who might cross your path again.

Early in my training career, a boy of mine, let's call him Travis, had an idea to start an elite team of trainers. His vision was to spread the word around Jersey and use our collective skills to bring his brand to the forefront. At first, his idea sounded great. We were all hungry, ambitious, and willing to put in the work, but after a few months, it became clear that our end goals weren't in alignment. Some of the trainers had different aspirations, and the team eventually disbanded. Some walked away from the situation in a negative way by burning bridges, talking down on the opportunity, or resenting the outcome.

I didn't see the need for that.

At the end of the day, we all came together to try and build something, and even though it didn't pan out, it wasn't a failure. It was merely a lesson in alignment. Travis and I had known each other since middle school, and I respected his vision enough to consider being a part of it in the first place, so why would I tarnish our relationship just because we didn't share the same long-term goals? That would've been unnecessary.

To this day, Travis and I still encourage each other in our different lanes. We might not have built that elite training team together, but we still recognize and respect each other's grind. And that's the point. Just because a business partnership doesn't work out doesn't mean the relationship has to turn sour. You never know where life will lead you or who might cross your path again. Staying professional and maintaining respect keeps doors open that you may need in the future.

Think of it this way: Every relationship and interaction is a bridge. You don't have to cross every bridge every day, but if you burn the bridge, that's one less path you have the option of taking when you're navigating through life. So, keep those bridges strong, even if you don't use them daily.

POURING INTO CONNECTIONS WITHOUT EXPECTING A RETURN

I'm big on sharing energy and building people up, not for what they can do for me but because that's who I am. And that kind of mindset has brought blessings my way that I couldn't have planned for if I tried.

When you pour into business relationships—sharing knowledge, connecting people, or simply being there to support without expecting anything in return—it creates an environment where reciprocity flows naturally.

I remember when I helped someone who wasn't directly connected to my business. I gave them advice, shared resources, and did what I could to support them. Months down the line, that same person recommended me to someone in their network, which led to an unexpected and valuable business opportunity. That's why I emphasize being a giver. Not everything needs to be a calculated move with an immediate benefit.

In business and in life, your reputation precedes you. Build connections with authenticity and understand that every interaction has the potential to shape your future in ways you can't imagine. Keep showing up, keep being real, and keep building those connections that can elevate you to the next level.

CHAPTER THIRTEEN: TURNING SETBACKS INTO SETUPS

Coming off the importance of surrounding yourself with the right people, let's get real for a moment. No matter how strong your support system is or how motivated you feel, life will hit you when you least expect it. Your circle can push you, motivate you, and open doors, but when life tests you, it's just you, your will, and the battle in front of you. Setbacks don't care how ready you think you are or how strong your network is. Life's punches come in hard and without warning, testing your character and your grit. But here's the thing. They're not just obstacles. They're setups in disguise to see if you're willing to turn them into a comeback.

PART I: REFRAMING FAILURE AS OPPORTUNITY

Failure has this sneaky way of making you feel like you're at rock bottom. But failure is never the end. In fact, it's data. And guess what? Failure will be your greatest teacher if you learn how to listen. The brain is wired to avoid pain and seek safety and comfort, which is why failure feels so final. But in reality, failure is life's way of giving you a reality check and asking, "How bad do you want it?"

Let's break it down. Neuroplasticity, the brain's ability to rewire itself, kicks in when you push through failure. It's like your mind is in training mode, finding new pathways, and unlocking higher levels. So, the "how bad do you want it" question is actually backed by science. And here's some philosophy for you: German philosopher Friedrich Nietzsche said, "What does not kill us makes us stronger." That's real talk. The people you look up to, the legends who've made it, don't have a perfect track record of wins. No, they have failures stacked high, but they didn't let those failures bury them; they used them as steppingstones to grow and ultimately achieve greatness.

SHIFTING YOUR MINDSET ABOUT FAILURE

Changing how you view failure isn't a switch you flip. I know how easy it is to look at a setback and think, "Maybe I'm not cut out for this." Your brain holds on to negative experiences longer than positive ones thanks to something called negativity bias. Back when survival depended on remembering dangers, this bias was useful, but today, it can trap you in self-doubt.

You need to train your mind to see failure as another steppingstone, not a dead end. If you conquer this battle, you'll become nearly unstoppable. Failure isn't fatal unless you let it. It's up to you whether to look at failure and say, "Alright, I see what you're doing here, but I'm not staying down."

LESSONS HIDDEN IN DEFEAT

Let's get raw for a minute. It's not about the fall but what you learn when you're down. When my business took a hit after moving to Orlando, I felt a crushing weight of doubt. I started questioning everything.

Was this the right move?

Do I really have what it takes?

That transition stripped me of comfort and made me face raw reality. But here's the thing. If I hadn't experienced that transition, I wouldn't have re-evaluated, re-strategized, and come back better. That setback was my setup, plain and simple. It showed me the flaws in my approach and the places where I was getting too comfortable and pushed me to level up.

Well-known author and psychologist Dr. Angela Duckworth's research on grit explains it best: It's not talent that makes people great, it's resilience. It's the choice to stand back up after being knocked down, over and over again.

HOW TO REFRAME FAILURE IN YOUR LIFE

I'm not just telling you how to see failure differently, but I'm telling you how to do it. Start by committing to pulling yourself out of the emotional spiral. When you're deep in failure, emotions make everything feel ten times heavier. You need to separate who you are from what happened. You're not your failure. Failure is an event, not your identity. Say that again if you need to: Failure is an event, not my identity.

Find the lesson, even if it's hard. Ask yourself, "What is this moment teaching me?" Maybe it's pointing out a weakness you didn't know you had or showing you where you need to shift gears. Whatever it is, don't just see it. Act on it and keep moving. The longer you stay down, the harder it is to get up. Analyze, learn, and push forward. Setbacks will be the reason you stop or the reason you climb higher. The choice is yours.

PART II: STRATEGIES FOR BOUNCING BACK

Setbacks are inevitable, but staying down is optional. This isn't just about getting up, it's about how you get up and what you do differently when you're back on your feet. Anyone can fall, but only the relentless find ways to rise smarter, stronger, and hungrier. Here's what you need to know about making your comeback count.

Step 1: Pause and acknowledge. Before you jump back into action, pause and take stock of what happened. Too many people rush back into the game without assessing the play that went wrong. That's not grit. That's foolish. Pausing doesn't mean giving in to defeat. It means respecting the lesson. Sit in the discomfort for a moment to understand it. Acknowledge what didn't go your way, and don't sugarcoat the truth. If you messed up, own it. If circumstances outside your control knocked you down, admit that, too. Acknowledge, assess, and get ready to adjust.

I've had moments where I rushed through failures, thinking I could outwork my mistakes. It took me longer than I'd like to admit to realize that rushing doesn't fix what's broken. You've got to be brutally honest with yourself about what went wrong before you can fix it.

Step 2: Analyze without judgment. This step is crucial. You need to go through what happened with a critical eye but without judging yourself. The point isn't to beat yourself up but to find the gaps and address them.

Were you unprepared?

Did you underestimate the challenge?

Did your pride get in the way?

This is the moment to acknowledge hard truths. The comeback isn't just about raw energy. It's about calculated moves and sharp strategy.

Think about it like training. When you're working on a specific skill, you don't just move blindly. Instead, you analyze your form, adjust, and repeat. Life's no different. Dissect your setbacks with that mindset.

Step 3: Rebuild with precision. The greatest comebacks are built on deliberate actions. Once you've analyzed the situation, rebuild smarter. This is where the grind meets strategy. It's easy to say you'll work harder, but working harder without intention is a one-way ticket to burnout. Now is the time to set micro-goals and knock them down one by one.

I remember when I faced one of my most brutal setbacks after moving to Orlando. Business was slow, and I felt like I was losing my edge. I knew going harder wasn't enough. I had to rethink my entire approach, reconnect with my purpose, and get tactical about my comeback. I set daily objectives that brought me closer to the bigger picture, whether it was securing one new client each week or booking one speaking engagement a month. Little by little, those micro-wins compounded into significant progress, turning my goals into reality.

SURROUND YOURSELF WITH RESILIENCE

Surrounding yourself with people who push you to bounce back is essential. These are the ones who don't just pat you on the back and say, "It's going to be okay," but the ones who say, "Alright, what's the plan?" When I struggled, my circle was there to remind me why I started. They challenged me to push beyond my limits and held me accountable.

If you're going through a setback, don't isolate. Lean on your people, those who push you, challenge you and refuse to let you give up. And if you don't have those people? It's time to find them or become that person for yourself. Resilience thrives in community. Iron sharpens iron.

THE SCIENCE AND PHILOSOPHY OF BOUNCING BACK

I know I didn't go to college for an education. I went to escape, but don't get it twisted—I've always been sharp, even if my classroom was more of a gym than a lecture hall. So, let's dive into some P&P (Philosophical and Psychological) insight to break down why bouncing back isn't just about grit but about training your mind and soul to shift the narrative.

Resilience isn't a mere buzzword. It's a skill that comes from building a growth mindset, a term coined by psychologist Carol Dweck.

People with a growth mindset believe their abilities can be developed through dedication and hard work. When they hit a setback, they see it as a step toward growth, not the end of the road. And here's the kicker: Your brain can rewire itself to think this way if you consistently practice it.

Fail, adapt, and grow.

Sounds straightforward, right?

Well, it's more like a daily uphill battle.

To be honest, I didn't know most of these philosophers by name. I had to look them up after coming across their quotes during my study sessions. But the lessons? Those stuck with me. Take Marcus Aurelius, an OG of stoicism. He said, "You have power over your mind, not outside events. Realize this, and you will find strength." Simple advice hits different when life decides to throw you into the deep end. This isn't just about dodging punches but about becoming a mental heavyweight who doesn't crumble when life comes swinging.

Did you know that cognitive reappraisal, a strategy used in cognitive-behavioral therapy, is all about reframing how you see negative experiences? It's proven to help people bounce back by looking at situations from a different perspective and finding a positive meaning. This mental framework builds resilience. You start looking at failures like plot twists in your own movie—setbacks that set up the comeback. That's when you start winning the battle in your head, one reframe at a time.

P&P AND YOU: APPLYING IT TO YOUR LIFE

How are you viewing your setbacks? Are they painful roadblocks or potential springboards? When you face something tough, is your first thought, "This is impossible," or "How do I flip this?" The power of reframing lies in practice. Start rewiring your mind to see setbacks as opportunities to play your best cards and emerge victorious.

PART III: THE COMEBACK MINDSET

A setback isn't the end of your story. It's a test, a gut check, to see how much fight you've got in you. The real champions are the ones who don't just take the hit but get back up, adjust, and come back with a plan. This mindset is what separates the average from the exceptional, the dreamers from the doers. I call it the Comeback Mindset.

Your mindset can turn failures into fuel. A comeback mindset is built on taking your losses and using them to build a launchpad. It's looking at failure and saying, "Alright, what's next? How do I use this to my advantage?" The key is seeing every stumble as a learning opportunity.

Grow through the grind. The comeback mindset isn't passive. It's active, raw, and relentless. It's waking up at 4 a.m. when every fiber in your body screams to stay in bed. It's putting in the work when no one's watching and reminding yourself why you started when the progress feels slow. Kobe Bryant once said, "Rest at the end, not in the middle."

That's the mindset of someone who's not just trying to be good but great. You can't let temporary discomfort make you forget your long-term vision.

Research on resilience shows that people who recover from setbacks the fastest are the ones who engage in problem-focused coping. This means they don't just sit with their feelings; they actively work to solve the problem at hand. The comeback mindset embodies this. Don't allow your emotions to drown you. Channel them into action.

Nobody is saying that bouncing back is easy. It's brutal. It's hard when life feels like it's stacking obstacles faster than you can knock them down. But those are the moments that reveal your character. I always say, "Life will test you to see how badly you actually want it." And when it does, you have two options: Let it break you or let it build you.

STEPS TO IMPLEMENT

1. **Reframe the narrative**: The first step is to control the story you're telling yourself. Instead of, "Why did this happen to me?" ask, "What can I learn from this?"
2. **Plan your comeback**: Take action. Set small, achievable goals that get you back on track.
3. **Stay consistent**: Remember that it's not only about the big moments but showing up every day. Build your resilience muscle.
4. **Lean on your support system**: Don't underestimate the power of the people around you. Let them remind you of who you are when life tries to make you forget.

5. **Reflect and adjust**: Take time to look back, not to dwell, but to learn and adapt for the future.

The mind is powerful, and the philosophy of stoicism teaches us to focus on what we can control. When setbacks hit, control your mindset. Own your comeback.

PART IV: HARNESSING RESILIENCE

The word "resilience" gets thrown around a lot, but what does it really mean? It's more than the ability to take hits and keep moving. It's about learning to leverage those hits to build yourself back up, stronger and wiser. Resilience is about mastering the art of recovery and making sure you're better for it.

I remember training a client who was on the verge of giving up. They had hit a plateau, their motivation was at an all-time low, and every session felt like a battle. It reminded me of moments in my own life when progress felt invisible, and every step forward seemed to come with two steps back. But I didn't let them quit. I showed them how to shift their perspective, to see that resilience isn't just about the significant milestones but the discipline of showing up. Together, we focused on daily wins—lifting a little more weight, showing up when the energy wasn't there, and making better meal choices. Soon enough, that client started to build momentum, realizing that resilience is built one decision at a time.

This was a powerful reminder to me as well that sometimes it's not your own journey that teaches you but guiding someone else through theirs. The determination and progress they showed made me realize that setbacks are opportunities to reinforce your strength. Stay in motion. Even if you're crawling, keep moving. Momentum isn't always about speed. It's about direction. When you're in motion, you're making progress. Celebrate each step and trust that they are leading you somewhere great.

Resilience doesn't come naturally to everyone, and that's okay. But you need to choose it over and over again. When I say resilience is non-negotiable, I mean it. Life will knock you down repeatedly, and each time, it'll whisper, "Stay down." That's when you have to rise up and shout back, "Not today."

Studies show that people who practice cognitive flexibility, the ability to shift their perspective and see different angles of a challenge, are better at bouncing back. It's about thinking strategically. When a door closes, resilience helps you find the window or break down the wall if need be.

If life has you questioning your strength or making you feel like you've lost your way, I'm here to tell you that resilience is in you. It's a muscle waiting to be trained. Marcus Aurelius said, "The impediment to action advances action. What stands in the way becomes the way." Take this with you: When setbacks come, don't avoid them. Face them head-on, full steam ahead.

PART V: THE COMEBACK BLUEPRINT

Setbacks can feel like the end, but they're just another chapter in your story, and you hold the pen. This section is about crafting a blueprint that turns every setback into a setup for a comeback. This is a practical guide for forging a forward path when the ground beneath you feels unstable.

Identify the lessons: Every setback carries lessons that are easy to miss when you're focused on the pain. Take time to reflect and ask yourself what this situation is teaching you. Did you get too comfortable? Did you ignore a red flag? This honest assessment isn't about self-blame but building awareness so you can move forward smarter and more prepared.

Rebuild with intention: After identifying the lessons, it's time to start rebuilding with a clearer sense of purpose. This means creating a plan that focuses on your strengths but acknowledges where you fell short. Maybe you need to sharpen a skill, build a new habit, or remove distractions. Your comeback plan should be realistic and specific, outlining actionable steps to take each day to get back on track.

Mindset matters: Your mindset is critical. It's easy to get caught up in the "what-ifs" and "should-haves," but regret is a chain that keeps you tied to the past. Instead, adopt what I like to call constructive reflection. It's looking back just enough to learn but not so long that it paralyzes you.

Stay grounded: Surround yourself with friends and mentors who won't just cheer you on but will also check you when you're struggling. The power of your circle isn't just for the good times. They're in your life to help you when your journey gets tough, and your vision starts to blur.

Reflection
- What setback in your life is currently teaching you a valuable lesson?
- How can you create a comeback plan that incorporates what you've learned?
- Who in your circle can you lean on to help you stay grounded and accountable?

Remember that the comeback isn't just about proving others wrong but proving yourself right. It's showing up for the person you're becoming, even when that path is full of detours.

PART VI: WHY MOST PEOPLE QUIT

Let's face a harsh truth. Most people give up because they can't handle the discomfort of growth. It's easier to quit than to endure the relentless pursuit of excellence. It's easier to settle than to push through the days when nothing seems to go your way. But the moment you decide to quit, you give up on more than just a goal; you give up on the person you could become.

One of the most common reasons people quit is because they overestimate how quickly success should come. We live in a world that glorifies instant results, so when we don't get what we want as fast as we think we should, discouragement creeps in. It's not that people aren't capable of greatness. It's that they haven't learned to stay patient and trust the process. I've seen this happen to friends and people I've trained and coached. They started strong, fueled by the initial rush of motivation, but when the grind set in and results began to slow down, their commitment wavered.

If you're considering quitting, ask yourself, "Am I willing to let this dream go and settle for what I have now?" Because that's the trade-off. Fight through the discomfort, setbacks, and doubts, or you stay where you are. And if you choose to stay, you need to be honest with yourself about what that means.

WHY MOST PEOPLE QUIT

Philosopher Marcus Aurelius said, "You have power over your mind, not outside events. Realize this, and you will find strength." This resonates deeply with why people give up. Too often, the focus is on what we can't control—circumstances, timing, and setbacks. But true strength lies in mastering your reaction to those circumstances. When you stop trying to control everything outside of yourself and focus on resilience within, quitting becomes less of an option.

The human brain is wired to avoid discomfort and seek safety, which is why enduring the grind is so difficult. The amygdala, a part of the brain responsible for processing emotions such as fear, reacts to challenging situations by triggering a fight-or-flight response. This is why, when things get hard, a person's first instinct is often to run, quit, and retreat to what feels safe. But growth requires you to override that instinct. Pushing through requires tapping into your prefrontal cortex, the part of your brain responsible for decision-making and rational thinking, by reminding yourself why you started and what's at stake if you quit.

Consider practicing cognitive reframing. When you feel like giving up, catch yourself and reframe your thoughts. Instead of thinking, "This is too hard," tell yourself, "This challenge is making me stronger." Shifting the narrative in your mind trains your brain to associate discomfort with growth, not defeat.

Reflection

- What's your why? (Remember that you have a big "why" that drives your overall choices and purpose, as well as a daily "why," which is what you'll achieve today.) Is your "why" strong enough to carry you through the hard days?
- Are you willing to confront your fear head-on and push through it?
- Can you commit to seeing the process through, even when progress feels slow?

CHAPTER FOURTEEN: LIVING THE EXCUSE KILLER LIFESTYLE

BRINGING IT ALL TOGETHER: THE NO EXCUSE PHILOSOPHY

Living the Excuse Killer lifestyle isn't just a mantra. It's my reality. This isn't something I read in a book or learned in a seminar. It's what I had to live through, scrape through, and fight tooth and nail for when every reason to quit stared me dead in the eyes. When I talk about living without excuses, this message comes from a kid from East Orange who felt the weight of life pressing down so hard that he almost didn't make it out.

LIVING WITHOUT EXCUSES: THE MINDSET AND PRACTICE

Life didn't get easier after the day I almost took my life. The pain just shifted. I fell into cycles of numbing the hurt, turning to lean, alcohol, porn, or anything to escape the reality that I wasn't living up to who I knew I could be. I didn't want to face myself because the truth hurt too much. When my father passed away, I hit rock bottom. Seeing him lifeless, knowing I'd never hear his voice again, shattered me in a way I can't fully explain.

It wasn't just that moment but a culmination of situations. Suicidal thoughts came back but more intense. I questioned my worth, my purpose, and whether life was worth fighting for anymore. A battle was raging inside my mind, but every time I thought I couldn't take another step, a tiny flicker within me refused to die. I realized I couldn't keep hiding behind excuses, blaming my circumstances or the cards I'd been dealt. If I wanted anything to change, I had to own every mistake, failure, and choice that got me here.

INSPIRING OTHERS TO CUT THE EXCUSES

Let me be clear. I'm not perfect, and I never will be, but I am relentless. I don't share this to paint myself as some hero who figured it all out. I'm telling you this because I know what it feels like to be at the edge. I know what it's like to try to drink the pain away and numb yourself until you feel nothing, only to wake up feeling emptier than before. I know what it's like to look in the mirror and hate the person staring back, to feel the weight of all your failures pressing down on you. But you don't have to keep running from yourself or let the past dictate who you are. It's not about being flawless but showing up, even when it hurts. It's about healing, not for anyone else, but for you.

Living without excuses means facing brutal truths, such as instances when you have hurt other people, the moments you took the easy way out, and the days when you chose comfort over growth. It's being honest enough to admit when you've made a mistake but determined enough to fix it.

PERSONAL REFLECTION AND CALL TO ACTION

I'm not here to judge you or preach to you. I've been at rock bottom, and I've made more mistakes than I can count. I've lied, hurt people, and betrayed my integrity more times than I'd like to admit. But here's the thing: those moments don't define me. They refined me, and I want you to understand that this fight, this life, is worth your time and energy. You're not alone, and your pain isn't pointless. It prepares you for what's to come, for the battles that only you can fight and win.

Be real with yourself. Don't hide from the hurt. Embrace your feelings, learn from them, and use them as fuel. You've got what it takes. You've made it this far, and that's proof that you're stronger than you think.

A LETTER TO MY SISTER

To my sister, Clarise Simmons, the strongest soldier I know. You stood tall when the world felt like it was caving in on us. You held our father's hand and prayed with him during his last breath, and in that moment, I saw a level of strength that words can't capture. You convinced me not to drop out of college when everything inside me wanted to run and quit. You kept me grounded, and for that, I owe you so much. Thank you for taking care of Mom when I moved to pursue my dream, even when I was so locked into my grind that my communication fell short. You loved me through it all, supported me, and never wavered. I vow to pay back that type of love and loyalty in everything I do. You are my hero.

A LETTER TO MY MOTHER

Mom, Tracey Simmons, you have shown me what unconditional love truly looks like. Even when we were at odds, your love never faded. Thank you for listening to me, not just as a son who made mistakes but as a son who learned from them. You've carried so much weight, especially after Dad passed, and still keep love in your heart. You made our house a home, even when life tried to shatter it. Thank you for your sacrifices, strength, and unwavering belief in me. I vow to work hard every day to make sure you live comfortably, to retire you, and to give you back far more than what you've given me. You are my foundation, and I love you beyond words.

A LETTER TO MY FATHER

Dad, Randolph Simmons Sr., thank you for the lessons, the fights, the experiences, and the love. Thank you for making the decision to be a father, not just a man who brought a child into this world. You used your struggles and the harsh lessons you learned to mold me and prepare me for a world that doesn't give handouts. Thank you for instilling discipline, teaching me that winning isn't given but earned, and showing me that real strength comes from within. I wish I could see you one last time to tell you that I love you and to thank you face to face. I hope you're proud of who I've become, and I pray that I get to experience your presence in Heaven. Until then, I'll carry your lessons in my heart every day.

TO THE READER

To you, the reader, thank you. Thank you for taking the time to read this book, investing in your growth, and for your interest in becoming an Excuse Killer. Your time is valuable, and I don't take that for granted. Choosing to finish this book means more to me than words can express. Time is something we never get back, and the fact that you spent yours with me on these pages is an honor I hold close. I encourage you to share this book with those you love, to spread the lessons and the mindset that have helped me climb out of dark places and push forward. You are not alone on this journey, and my hope is that these words serve as a reminder of your power and potential. From the bottom of my heart, thank you. Thank you for stepping up, for wanting to be better, and for committing to cutting the excuses from your life. This journey isn't easy, but it's worth it, and I'm proud of you for choosing to walk it. From the Excuse Killer himself, Randy NoExcuse, I love you. Together, let's shout, "No Excuse."

A LETTER TO GOD

Dear God, first and foremost, thank You. Thank You for being my Guide, my Anchor, and my Everything. Without Your relentless love and mercy, I wouldn't be standing here today. You saved me when I didn't think I deserved saving. You gave me strength when I was at my weakest, and You showed me the way forward when I felt completely lost. Thank You for carrying me through the battles that nearly broke me and for molding me into the man I am becoming.

Lord, I pray over this book and every person who decides to pick it up. Let these words be more than ink on a page. Let them be a light, a beacon of hope, and a spark that ignites change. For those who are struggling, lost, or questioning their path, I ask that You make Your presence known in their lives. Even if they don't believe in You yet, I pray that they feel something, Your peace or Your comfort, so they know they're not walking this journey alone.

Bless them, Lord. Grant them resilience for the hard days, courage when they feel like giving up, and hope when life feels overwhelming. Let this book remind them that healing is possible, that strength is built in the deepest struggles, and that they are so much more capable than they might think.

If this book can touch just one life, if it can make one person feel seen, heard, and understood, then it was worth every sleepless night, every painful memory, and every lesson learned. Let these pages speak truth, and let that truth be louder than any lie or excuse they've held onto.

Thank You for choosing me, a kid from East Orange who had every reason to give up but didn't, to carry this message. Thank You for trusting me to be a vessel for Your truth, for showing me that even in my lowest moments, You were preparing me for this purpose. May Your name be lifted through these pages, and may this book serve as a testament to Your grace and the power You give us to keep pushing forward.

In Jesus' name, Amen.

Made in the USA
Columbia, SC
26 April 2025